The Splendid Mrs McCheyne

and the
East London Federation
of Suffragettes

JANE McCHRYSTAL

The Choir Press

Copyright © 2020 Jane McChrystal

All rights reserved. No part of this publication may be reproduced or transmitted in any form or by any means, electronic or mechanical including photocopying, recording or any information storage or retrieval system, without prior permission in writing from the publishers.

The right of Jane McChrystal to be identified as the author of this work has been asserted by her in accordance with the Copyright, Designs and Patents Act 1988.

First published in the United Kingdom in 2020 by
The Choir Press.

ISBN 978-1-78963-163-0

Contents

Who was Rosaline McCheyne?	1
Important Sources of Information	6
Transcript of an Interview with Anne Padfield, descendant of Rosaline McCheyne	8
Rosaline McCheyne: Commentary on an interview with her descendant, Anne Padfield	32
Article 1: She Carried on in the Most Splendid Way...	57
Article 2: Rosaline McCheyne: Coming of Age	61
Article 3: Rosaline McCheyne and the Street Where She Lived	63
Article 4: Rosaline and Herbert	67
Article 5: On the Home Front with Rosaline	69
Article 6: A Day in the Life of an Activist in 1914	73
Article 7: Woman's May Day, 24 May, 1914	77
Afterword	79

Who was Rosaline McCheyne?

I first came across her name in the minutes of ELFS' (East London Federation of Suffragettes) committee meetings during a stint as a volunteer researcher for the **Women's Hall Exhibition** staged at the Tower Hamlets Local History Library and Archive in 2018. The minutes showed that she attended regularly between 1913-16, but rarely contributed to the proceedings. If she wasn't the most vocal member, why did she go to meetings so frequently and what did she do for the Federation in between?

The results of some initial enquiries proved intriguing. The 1911 census revealed that Rosaline's husband, Herbert, was a woodwork teacher, a position which would have provided him with a steady income and adequate means to support a wife and family. The census also showed that Rosaline lived with Herbert, their three children, Robert, Georgina and Donald and one lodger at 55 Fairfield Road, Bow, in a decent three-storey early Victorian house which stands there to this day.

These circumstances suggest a comfortable lower-middle class way of life, very different to the lives of many other women in Bow who would have struggled to bring up enormous families in overcrowded homes on meagre wages in the early years of the twentieth century.

Rosaline could easily have absorbed herself in the many duties entailed in bringing up a family and managing a household and no one would have expected her to go beyond the domestic sphere at that time. So, why did she turn into an activist for women and what did she do?

While I was learning more about the facts of Rosaline's life and the social history of her era, one of her descendants, Anne Padfield, was doing some research of her own, and we got in touch after she emailed a question about her ancestor to the Tower Hamlets local history library. We met up to share our findings and reflections on what we knew about Rosaline which were recorded later in an interview with Anne and transcribed in part one of this collection.

We can never know what went on in Rosaline's mind but, as Anne suggested in the interview, she must have been moved to action by the plight of so many women in her neighbourhood. With no indoor sanitation it was impossible for them to keep on top of dirt and infestation in the home which resulted in shocking levels of disease and mortality among both adults and children.

Their men laboured hard in the docks and factories for low wages in dangerous conditions. Men were employed when work was available and when they were laid off or injured their wives went out charring or did piece-work at home.

The terrible deprivation Rosaline witnessed was the outcome of over one hundred years of intensive industrialisation in the East End, coupled with an enormous increase in the population. The process began with the construction of the docks along the Thames and on the Isle of Dogs, which made London the trading heart of the British Empire. Shipbuilders expanded their yards and the iron makers arrived to supply the materials they needed. Numerous other industries followed to add more filth to the noxious, sooty air East Enders breathed every day.

People flocked from all over England, Scotland and Ireland in search of work and speculators rushed to throw up the rickety tenements and mean terraces which became their homes. Seafarers from all over the world – Asia, Africa, China and the Caribbean – landed in the docks and some stayed. Between 1881 and 1914 one hundred and twenty thousand Jewish refugees joined them, in flight from the pogroms unleashed across the Russian Empire by the assassination of Czar Alexander II.

Not everyone was desperate. Someone had to supply food, drink and services to the local population, no matter how deprived it was; the East End needed its grocers, butchers, publicans and tobacconists, many of whom would have been local residents.

Some grander individuals built their homes close to where their employees lived, and the substantial villas in locations like Tredegar Road, Bow, are a reminder of their presence in the East End. The Green family of Poplar donated the profits from their ship yards in Blackwall to a number of philanthropic enterprises in the area, such as the George Green School, which still educates children on the Isle of Dogs with support from the Worshipful Company of Shipwrights.

Philanthropists were drawn in from outside, attracted by the opportunity to relieve misery and look for new recruits to their cause.

The Methodist missionaries, who arrived in the East End in 1843, were determined to recruit the many seafarers who lived in the vicinity of the Port of London and save them from the boozers and brothels which crowded the streets of Sailor Town around the Ratcliff Highway. Their pious talk of spreading spiritual uplift and promoting moral welfare might sound patronising to us, but sailors on a spree after months at sea were often fathers of families in urgent need of their pay. Their work has endured and the mission they established on the East India Road, now known as the Victoria Sea Men's Rest, still provides merchant seamen who have fallen on hard times with good hot meals, companionship, help with benefits and secure accommodation.

Radical thinkers visited from Russia and Germany in search of a proletariat ripe for revolution. However, the workers were organising from within to form the trade unions which were to play such a significant role in the history of British labour.

In 1888 the women and girls of the Bryant and May factory went on strike and against all the odds won their demands for better pay and conditions. They also forced the factory owners to substitute red for the yellow phosphorous in the manufacture of matches to save themselves from the risk of developing "phossy jaw", a horrible disease which caused the disintegration of the jaw. A year later the Dockers' unions won the right to less precarious terms of employment and a minimum rate of sixpence per hour or the "docker's tanner" which became the popular tag for their strike.

In 1912 another home-grown radical, George Lansbury, contested the Election in Bromley and Bow on the Votes for Women ticket. He lost, but his campagn had another important consequence: Sylvia Pankhurst arrived in the East End to support Lansbury. In 1913 she set up an East End branch of the Women's Social and Political Union, the organisation founded by her mother Emmeline to fight for women's suffrage. Rosaline McCheyne joined this branch in 1913.

After a disagreement with her sister Christabel 1914, Sylvia parted company with the WSPU, moved to 400 Old Ford Road and made it the Headquarters of a new movement for women's suffrage, the East London Federation of Suffragettes. Rosaline was to become one of its most active members.

In piecing together Rosaline's story, a number of questions began to arise about what happened to her and her family and some of them were quite troubling.

Did Rosaline's children outlive her? Were her sons, Robert and Donald, conscripted to the armed forces in the First or Second World War? What was life like for her daughter, Georgina, after women won the vote? Did Rosaline live to see the social reforms which transformed the lives of people in the East End after the Second World War? How long did she have with Herbert in her life?

Luckily, Anne turned up with all the answers.

So now I can present you with everything I've learned about Rosaline.

I suggest you start with the interview with Anne, pages 8–31, which you can use to guide you to the commentary or the group of articles based on the research I carried out for the Women's Hall Exhibition.

You'll notice that the articles were not changed after the interview with Anne, even though I learned so much more about Rosaline from her. I hope the differences between them and the transcript will provide an insight into the way a project of this nature evolves as the investigator becomes more deeply involved with her subject.

The numbers in brackets on the pages of the interview will direct you to a note in the commentary, pages 32–56, or the collection of articles, pages 57–79, which also references which page in the interview the note appears on.

The commentary was designed to fill out the broader social history of the era Rosaline and her family lived through. Otherwise, just jump in wherever you please and take a wander – the important thing is to enjoy reading about Rosaline as much as I've enjoyed putting together my discoveries about her.

Important Sources of Information

Sarah Jackson and Rosemary Taylor's work "**East London Suffragettes**", published as part of the History Press's *Voices of History* series, was an indispensable point of reference.

You will see references to the *Woman's Dreadnought* throughout the interview, commentary and group of articles. This was a weekly newspaper launched by Sylvia Pankhurst and Zelie Emerson on the 21st March 1914, which was issued weekly until the final edition appeared 21st July 1917.

The *Woman's Dreadnought* was published to spread the word about the Federation's work and campaigns and document the hard lives of women in the East End. It is surprisingly internationalist in outlook, with its reports on women's struggle for equality in Europe and the USA, though maybe this is not so surprising in view of Sylvia's career in later life as an anti-colonialist campaigner in Ethiopia where she died in 1960.

The *Woman's Dreadnought*'s radical message attracted the attention of the police who frequently raided its offices and finding sales pitches where the *Woman's Dreadnought* could be sold unopposed was another challenge. Each copy cost one halfpenny but after the first four days of issue, any newspapers left over from the weekly print run of 20,000 were distributed for nothing.

Much of the copy was made up of reports of women and girls and their struggles at work and in the home illustrated by the photographs of Sylvia's companion Norah Smyth, which appeared in an exhibition of her work at the Four Corners Gallery (http://fourcornersfilm.co.uk/East-End-Suffragettes) in 2018. Norah's photographs were uncredited, so this recent exposure has brought them to the attention of a much wider audience and served to establish her as an important figure in the history of women's photography.

They can be viewed online on the website (socialhistory.org/en/news/east-end-suffragettes-photographs-norah-smyth-london) of the International Institute of Social History (IISH) where the originals are stored. They are also available at the Tower Hamlets Local History Library and Archive.

In 1917 the *Woman's Dreadnought* became the *Worker's Dreadnought* a year after ELFS was renamed the Workers' Suffrage Federation in order to embrace a wider mission; equality and social justice for all.

Anyone who joins the Tower Hamlets Local History Library and Archive can read and handle original copies of the *Woman's Dreadnought* with the librarians' permission which is an exciting experience but, to save wear and tear on these precious artefacts, you might consider consulting them online instead at: www.britishnewspaperarchive.co.uk/titles/womans-dreadnought

You will also see frequent references to the minutes of the ELFS meetings in all three parts of this work. They are available along with the rest of Sylvia's papers on the IISH at search.socialhistory.org/Record/ARCH01029/ArchiveContentList#A0da290c46c, where they appear as documents number 206-209. I must finish this preface to Rosaline's life and times by thanking my fellow research volunteer, Rosemary Lucas, who undertook the task of deciphering the hand-written notes to make them available in a legible form to the rest of the research team. Without her painstaking work I would never even have found Rosaline's name.

Transcript of an Interview with Anne Padfield, descendant of Rosaline McCheyne, Member of the East London Federation of Suffragettes 1913-1916, Tower Hamlets Local History Library and Archive, 29th October 2018

JMcC: Hello Anne, I'm Jane McChrystal, project volunteer with the Women's Hall Exhibition, interviewing you about your ancestor Rosaline McCheyne, member of the East London Federation of Suffragettes. (1) Perhaps you could start out by saying who you are.

AP: My name is Anne Padfield but my maiden name was Anne McCheyne and I'm a distant relative of Rosaline.

JMcC: OK, so you've had a chance to look at some of these questions about Rosaline, let's kick off with them. The first thing I'd like to ask you – when did you first become aware that you had a suffragette in the family?

AP: When I was a teenager I developed an interest in tracing my family tree – at that stage it was mainly just connecting names and dates and I discovered then that the lady I called my aunt, Georgina, said "Oh my mother was a suffragette" – and she told me one or two little stories about her and that's all I knew about her till quite recently.

JMcC: You've already mentioned that you're related to Rosaline – perhaps you could say how (2).

AP: More specifically my grandfather, Allan McCheyne, and Rosaline's husband, Herbert McCheyne, were first cousins. And he [Herbert] belonged to what you might call the town branch and my side of the family followed the tradition of farming in Scotland and then my great-grandfather [George] took the opportunity to come down from Scotland and farm in Essex as a lot of Scottish farmers did in about 1900. So, the two families ended up not too far apart.

JMcC: I think you might have mentioned that you had contact with one of Rosaline's close relatives – her daughter, I think?

AP: Yes, Georgina. Rosaline had three children, Robert known as Bob and later there was a long gap. Eleven years later, along came Georgina and her brother, Don, was born three years later. Georgina and her family and my family, when I was young were very close – we were second cousins by that stage but knew each other very well. Georgina and her family spent summer, Christmas and Easter holidays with us because we lived in a big farmhouse in the country and we'd see each other every Sunday. So, even though she was genealogically a bit distant they were actually very close friends as well as relatives.

JMcC: What was your impression of Georgina?

AP: She loved books and one of the things I loved, when I was a child, when she came to stay was that she read us bedtime stories, which my mother with four children didn't have time for. You could see from the way she read them – she savoured every word. She encouraged us to write poems. She was quite artistic. She was good at drawing and especially for dressmaking. It was her work. Before she had children, she worked as a lecturer at a technical college (1a) in Dagenham (1b). She taught people to make their own dress patterns and then during the Second World War there was the Make Do and

Mend Policy – and she taught how to turn an old coat into a waistcoat or a pair of slippers or something (1) we used to win all the fancy dress competitions locally because she made them all. So, she was a lovely lady, but she was quite selective about what she said about her background. Because although she was technically a cockney, I suppose, she was born in Bow, she always said she lived in London (2).

JMcC: Not too specific then.

AP: No, I think she – people in those days they presented themselves as being – being respectable was very important and so you just missed out the slightly less comfortable things.

JMcC: When we last spoke you mentioned that she had this London background but she used to spend holidays in Summer in Essex. Can you tell me a bit more about that?

AP: Yes, my great-grandfather [George] and then my grandfather [Allan] were farming in a place called Mountnessing Hall. Mountnessing is a village just the other side of Brentwood. So, it was really quite easy to get on a train, to get to Liverpool Street and I think they would have gone from Liverpool Street to somewhere like Shenfield, anyway relatively easy to get there. They lived in smoky, sooty old London and it was quite common, I think, for even quite young children to go out and spend holidays with granny or auntie or whoever it was out in the country. Well, first of all her much older brother Bob, he was a very frequent visitor at Mountnessing Hall, they treated him almost like another brother and then when Georgina and Don came along, he probably took them out there and they just led the same life as the family. Which was strange because of the different generations, there was a bit of slippage, so they were all actually older than her so she wasn't just there to play with other children – there were probably lots of other children in her street in Bow, weren't there? And so, she just lived the same kind of life, the farming life with the lovely big house with cows and horses. It was a good thing to do to send your children out to the healthy countryside.

JMcC: Different to what she would have experienced in Bow.

AP: Yes, I think she always felt more comfortable with country people. Well, she liked London and all the facilities, but I think she yearned for that side of the family. That was her selective side. The two girls who were, as I said, were ten and fifteen years older, she remained on good terms with them. She visited them much later, when she was married, and kept up with them. There was a lot of networking went on in these farming families. It seemed to be something they were very good at.

JMcC: Did Georgina ever talk to you about her mother's life as an activist in the East End?

AP: She only told me one story which did make an impression on me. She said "oh my mother was a suffragette" and, of course, I didn't ask enough questions as always. And she said she went to a demonstration once where Sylvia Pankhurst was addressing people and it was broken up by the police. But she wasn't too involved in it. She made it sound more like she was on the sidelines (1), and she said it was in the paper, it said something like "Mrs. McCheyne was uninjured". I've never found the paper that says that but you told me that you think you know which particular demonstration that was.

JMcC: Yes – it was a May Day demonstration possibly in 1914 and actually Rosaline did have a role in it in that she, she was on the sidelines so that when the police had broken up the demonstration and arrested the women who made up Sylvia's bodyguard – she went down to Bow Road Police Station and bailed them out.

AP: She had the money, so it was important that she didn't get arrested herself. And that was the only story she told me. Well I would have been so proud of my mother. But she mentioned it in a matter of fact way and then that was that.

JMcC: And it was quite a significant event as well.

AP: Yes it was and her [Georgina's] son, Iain, who I'm still in contact with, he'd never even heard that story and his mother never told or talked to him at all about her childhood. I knew more about it than he did.

I think that it was that thing about – not that she cultivated it – her best friends and contacts were our side of the family and the descendants of those at Mountnessing Hall, that was her social circle (1) and so to say you were actually born in Poplar and that kind of thing it was not quite the image she wanted to convey. I'm not saying that she was a great snob or anything but I think it was quite normal then. Even the working classes were anxious to be respectable and for people to be seen to be respectable. Maybe there was something a bit downmarket about living in Poplar and so she presented the, you know, "my father was in education" she said.

JMcC: Well that leads us on nicely to my next question. Did she talk about her father, Herbert?

AP: She did. She talked a little bit more about him than her mother, but again, very brief references. She often mentioned he was a teacher but it was quite difficult to prise out of her the fact that he was a woodwork teacher (1). He taught a practical subject, not an academic one, whereas she was such a lover of books and literature. In those days, you could get loads of books from the library. She loved Dickens and people's biographies and historical characters so whether she got that from her father or not – quite possibly either of them. Originally, he had a – his father was a chemist... not a very successful one. They kept going bankrupt. He [Georgina's father, Herbert] started off as something called a pattern maker – makes patterns for metal parts of machines out of wood – so it was quite precision carpentry and then that sort of led on, I suppose, to the – it was a London County Council school – I don't know which one, but I imagine it would have been whatever was the nearest one to home and he taught there.

JMcC: Isn't it interesting that he made patterns for metal machinery and then she...

AP: Yes, and much later, Georgina, she became a dress-maker's pattern maker. It is isn't it? So maybe he was good at technical drawing, I imagine and she was good at drawing although she was good at fashion drawings for dressmaking...

JMcC: The same kind of skills would be involved. So maybe she was just more interested in him and that might explain why...

AP: ... she identified more with him. I was able – I spoke to my mother actually yesterday – she does have memory problems, because she has Alzheimers – but sometimes memories will come back to her quite clearly and yesterday was quite a good day. She didn't meet Rosaline socially – she wouldn't have known her until she was an old lady, anyway. She [Anne Padfield's mother] married into the McCheyne family. She didn't meet her to speak to her socially but she met, she saw her at Rosaline's granddaughter's funeral. Georgina sadly had a little girl who died at six and she met Rosaline. So, I asked my mother a few questions about her but because she hadn't spoken to her too much, she [Anne Padfield's mother] had the impression that Georgina was quite supportive of Rosaline – she was much older by then and she needed to go round and do things for her and I said, you know, did they get on? So, she said "Oh yes, I think so". I wouldn't say they [Rosaline and Georgina] were close, close. They [Rosaline and Georgina] were on good terms and I got a feeling that she admired her father. Another thing she said about him – she didn't say he was an atheist but he was very sceptical about religion. Maybe he had an experience that put him off. She said he had a copy of the Bible and he used to write notes in the margin pointing out all the contradictions and impossibilities and, you know, you can imagine, that slightly narky attitude, and so I imagined him as a kind of – what you'd call nowadays a *Guardian*-reading liberal, so I was surprised to discover that he was active in the local Conservative Association which – Georgina never mentioned his politics – but I got the feeling she admired her father quite lot, but he died in the 1930s, whereas Rosaline lived to a great old age.

JMcC: I think you showed me some photographs the last time we met. Could you describe what you made of the photos?

AP: Yes, there were some photos taken in the '20s when Georgina she would have been in her early twenties and that's the only photograph that I have of Rosaline herself, but unfortunately she's wearing a great heavy fur, and she's wearing one of those cloche hats, so you can barely, she's wearing glasses and apart from that you can't . . . (1)

JMcC: But people did dress up then for a photo and having a fur stole would have been quite a status-symbol I think.

AP: Yes, oh absolutely, but it meant you could see very little of her [Rosaline's face], but the photograph you showed me, I found here in the ***Dreadnought***, her photograph as a committee member, and I found that very interesting. She has the same high cheek bones as Georgina and also she was sort of not looking straight at the camera, a bit uncomfortable about being photographed – a bit like Georgina – and so she would often slightly turn away (1). Perhaps that's my imagination but I thought I could see that in Rosaline as well. It sort of fits with her not pushing herself forward as well. She'd rather be useful in the background than be up front.

JMcC: Yes, this is the impression I've got of her. She was tremendously active, made a huge contribution to the work of the East London Federation of Suffragettes but somehow you never hear her voice. You don't see . . .

AP: She actually speaks about twice, recorded in the minutes anyway but what she does say is practical and common sense.

JMcC: Of course, we both know she played a part in every aspect of the work of the Federation. (2)

AP: Yes, of course. Georgina and Don were young at the time. So, you wonder how she fitted it all in.

JMcC: It's a big question and one we can't probably answer.

AP: I did notice that the minutes of the meeting show that the meetings were probably held in the afternoon or the early evening. People in those days, you know, working men, usually had their dinner at midday at home and so probably Herbert lived within walking distance of the house and he would come home for dinner and the women would spend all morning doing housework, cooking and sorting out anything else, so the afternoon was probably a little bit freer. I suspect that's when . . . Sylvia Pankhurst didn't have to think about housework or family responsibilities so she could probably organise things without having to take those things into account (1). So she [Rosaline] must have been very well organised to carry out her domestic duties and support the federation so strongly.

JMcC: Did you have any impression of what kind of character she was because you said you thought Herbert might have been a sort of *Guardian*-reading liberal. What about Rosaline?

AP: Yes. Initially I imagined him as a kind of liberal before I found out about his politics. I could imagine him being a bit of an awkward customer, pernickety, picking holes in the Bible, especially in those days, it would have been quite a radical thing to do and I imagined her as being quite a radical, teacherish person. Before marriage she was a post office sorting clerk. I think that was quite a respected job and you would have had to be well-organised and quite meticulous to do that, so that would have stood her in quite good stead for the admin and that kind of thing she did for the Federation (2). She did a lot of hands on stuff as well, didn't she, with the mothers and babies?

JMcC: That's what I was wondering, because the picture I was building of her was, maybe somebody quite warm and supportive maybe quite a motherly figure. I've just got that from the things that she did for the Federation.

AP: That might well be right – I just find it quite shadowy because each time I find out something about her it's not all in one direction.

So, I did at one point think she might have been quite a fierce teacherish person. I now think she was quite a lot more rounded than that and also she had to be quite brave, especially if she wasn't a sort of upfront person by nature, to sell the *Dreadnought* and to push for subscriptions and members.

JMcC: Which she was very good at – that's another thing that comes across in the minutes – her district was particularly good and she was noted for the good high numbers of *Dreadnought*s she was selling.

AP: More than some of the others.

JMcC: I don't think she would have stood for any nonsense, that's for sure, and I think the East End is very much like that today. You have to be assertive but not someone who comes across as stuck up or superior.

AP: If you start lecturing them or being too posh, yes because most of the members of the federation weren't the factory workers themselves because they didn't have time. They were the more middle-class sort of people who were doing it on their behalf. And I would describe her at the time as middle-class, lower middle-class.

JMcC: I have the impression of respectable lower middle-class.

AP: Yes.

JMcC: And I thought it was interesting because life was pretty restrictive for lower-middle-class women. You wouldn't exactly square that with going out on the street and campaigning.

AP: Oh, you mean socially restrictive. Maybe the town was different to the country because, as it happens, I've done quite a lot of research on my grandmother who married a McCheyne and I have her diaries for 1917 and 1918 – she gets on a train and goes up to London, usually with her sister and they'd drive the pony and trap to the station on their own, and they could be more free in the countryside.

JMcC: Actually, that was quite an important trend round about that period. Women were able to start going out and about on the street and travel without being thought about as "low" (1).

AP: Yes, a bit suspect, not quite respectable. Yeah.

JMcC: So, how did you find out that Rosaline's life was appearing as part of the Women's Hall exhibition?

AP: I think it was probably first in the "Who Do You Think You are Magazine" (2) I subscribe to, because of the family history thing and also the British Newspaper Archive. And they send you emails saying there's a lot more information being put online about the suffragettes because of the anniversary coming up. So, if you've researched an ancestor in the past, look again. So that's exactly what I . . . So I thought in a newspaper she would always have appeared as Mrs. McCheyne. So, I looked up Mrs. McCheyne in the Newspaper Archive (3) and I found the *Woman's Dreadnought* had just been put up on its database and all sorts of things popped up about Mrs. McCheyne. She was doing this, that and the other. She was selling **Dreadnoughts.** You could apply to her to go on a demonstration and so on. It was interesting. So I thought I'll just google her full name, and when I did, up popped the Tower Hamlets Women's Hall Exhibition and your piece on Rosaline McCheyne and I suddenly realised there was a whole lot more information than I'd thought.

JMcC: I think that's really interesting for anybody who's interested in pursuing their family history. The sheer joy of just coming across things unexpectedly. It pops up and the way we couldn't have looked for information in this way before.

AP: So now you have to keep looking back because so much more information keeps coming up on the internet.

JMcC: I think it's very interesting you were saying Georgina was always saying "Oh, Father was a teacher" but nowadays we just go and look at something like Ancestry.com and we know exactly what Herbert was (1).

AP: You could present a pretty false image if you wanted. You could tweak the information and no one would know otherwise, unless it was by chance.

JMcC: But now it's out there for everyone to see.

AP: Yes, you can get checked on quite easily to see if you're telling the truth. And yes, she was telling the truth but a nicer version.

JMcC: Although I can't see a problem with with being a woodwork teacher, it just didn't fit with her.

AP: Because she was interested in literature, poetry and that sort of thing she liked to give the impression he was more on the academic side of things, and that he was good at keeping discipline she said. He didn't have problems keeping discipline. I think he just taught boys, but then as my mother said woodwork class was a treat, particularly for difficult boys who were not academic, they would look forward to woodwork class because they would probably think "this is the sort of thing I can really do". I think he probably was really a good teacher and quite respected for it. So, she was right to be proud of him.

JMcC: I think what's come out so far is that there's quite a few mysteries around – things that don't square, that are quite shadowy.

I thought we might just have a chat about that now. I mean you and I were very interested in her level of involvement in the federation – just how much she was doing.

AP: Yes, you do wonder how she fitted it all in. Was she terribly well organised? I do wonder what she did about child care, because when she first started Georgina was born in 1907. Bob was much older and could be more independent as a teenager, but she was first involved – was it in 1913 or 1914 – Georgina was seven and Don was four. Well, if you've got a four-year-old . . . Did she take him along?

JMcC: Well you could go to school when you were four then. The other thing you mentioned, there were relatives – in the same road or close by?

AP: Yes, not too far away Herbert's elder brother, Ernest, well he was known as Ernest, he was one of those people who used his middle name, he had two daughters, Edna and Alice, they were born a little before Georgina in 1902 and 1904. Sadly, both their parents died – one in 1908 and then one in 1912. They were basically – they were orphaned in 1912. At that time I think Don, he was one or two, and Georgina was five, and I'm quite surprised the children ended up in a children's home and I thought well that's strange they only lived a few streets away. Why didn't Rosaline take them in? Particularly as in her own family, her parents adopted a much younger child, presumably from difficult circumstances or from a relative – it wasn't formal then (1). I often wondered why. But strangely they're – one of them I've been in contact with, a granddaughter who said "oh Edna used to love going out to Mountnessing". Georgina knew them. She knew the names of another pair of boy cousins. Herbert's sister had two boys, they probably also went to Mountnessing

Hall. I think Great-Grandfather was quite a generous man. It was an accepted thing to do then. It was a big house. So, I often wondered – she was so kind to all these East End mothers and yet her own nieces were struggling.

JMcC: Yes, it is puzzling. In my own family and friends' families – so many people were orphaned in those days and would just be automatically taken in by the closest relatives.

AP: And, although Rosaline had three children of her own, one of them quite young, in terms of the East End that was not a particularly a full household and two little girls would have probably helped with the housework and been quite an asset. They both actually went into domestic service and they stayed in domestic service all their lives.

JMcC: Now, obviously Rosaline couldn't have relied then on the relatives she'd lost to take care of the children. Was there anyone else around she might have been able to leave them with, so she could get on with her activities?

AP: There could well have been neighbours that could have helped out when she needed it.

JMcC: I'm just thinking, when I grew up in the East End, even in the 1960s, people would help each other out, if someone had to go into hospital or somebody had to go away unexpectedly.

AP: Yes, a neighbour would just take one child and the other would go somewhere else. I think that would have happened a lot and I can imagine that happening, but perhaps not so much on a regular basis for those [ELFS committee] meetings or going to the Bromley Office, which wasn't the closest one to where she lived. It would have been quite a commitment for her and I'm sure the children didn't just sort of – I don't know what school hours were then – Herbert would have been quite available – I don't know if men were supposed to do childcare in those days – I don't think they did.

JMcC: I think even until fairly recently many men wouldn't have wanted to have been seen pushing a pram.

AP: Even when my children were small, if a man brought a child to play group it was quite startling . . . but you know Herbert he would have been there at dinner time, and then he probably worked relatively short hours and he would have had the school holidays. So at least they were safe in the house if he was there – even if he was just reading the paper or whatever he was doing.

JMcC: Another thing is, I think, the man of the house would always expect tea on the table.

AP: Definitely tea on the table. She had to juggle all that with her suffragette activities as well which is quite . . .

JMcC: Well, now one of the biggest mysteries we came across was this sudden departure from the East London Federation in 1916 after two years of very intense activity. There's an article in the *Dreadnought* thanking her for all her hard work, how splendidly she carried on (**Article 1**) as they put it. And then the minutes of the meeting show something a bit different to her story that she was leaving the area . . .

AP: . . . she had to give up her work because she was leaving the area, which was a very acceptable way of resigning, because you know it wasn't because she wanted to resign or she was forced to resign. Then – but she didn't move. She didn't move until 1925.

JMcC: Yes, it was a long time wasn't it?

AP: Yes, ten years later. And she even went to a couple of meetings after she resigned. But then if she had intended to move – they were planning to move and then it fell through for some reason – although it would all have been rented property I would have thought – it was much easier to move then than it is now – people, local people would have seen her, her former friends, they would have known either that it was just an excuse or, yes, to cover up what?

JMcC: Would you like to speculate?

AP: Several different things, I think. Either she was working so hard, you know like burnout really. She was doing so much. Well, you know, enough is enough. Maybe Herbert said "enough is enough" or she was one of those people who, you know, it's all or nothing and they can't say no to being asked to do things. Maybe that was one reason. She might have fallen out with . . .

JMcC: There were lots of fallings out.

AP: Yes, there were, I notice there were others saying "I can't work with so and so, move her to another district". Another one that I thought of as well was that, at this time things seem to be starting to begin unravelling a little bit, in that initially, you know, you're full of enthusiasm and everybody . . . they start getting money worries and they say you know each branch has to make itself financially self-sufficient and that's a lot of pressure. And I couldn't quite work it out, but some organisers got paid and others didn't. Speakers got paid. Rosaline wasn't a speaker. People who were paid were encouraged, if they didn't need the money, to give some of it back and then there was a spate of friction and people being moved, and I'm wondering if she thought "hmm, no this isn't for me, it's all getting a bit ragged". And I think Sylvia's politics were getting more and more radical at that time and she thought, "well yes, while you're helping people in genuine need, I'm fine with that but I'm not sure about this more radical [. . .]paigning". I think she was pushing them to do more and more, maybe it was the chalking – was that writing slogans? There was a lot of chalking, yes, because they would have to buy chalk and she's saying, you know, "you must" (1), because they had a stall didn't they in a market . . .

JMcC: Yes, on Roman Road.

AP: I'm not sure if Rosaline was involved in that? I don't think so . . . I'm just wondering if she thought "this isn't quite moving the way I wanted".

JMcC: I think you've picked up on something because the Federation turned into a part of the labour movement in the end, part of the growing Labour Party, and obviously, round here with the docks, trade unionism was born in places like the East End and there was the first dockers' strike here (2). And quite a lot of ELFS' members were involved with or were married to men who were working in the docks. It just seemed like there was less interest in women and more in the conditions of labour and housing in the East End. I suppose one of the things I noticed about Rosaline was the family's position, with a man bringing in a steady wage with a good job. He was not getting laid off and there were no periods with no money coming in. That was quite different to a lot of the other women involved. So, maybe this move towards radicalisation and the labour movement, was something that she wasn't so interested in.

AP: Yeah, it could be and it's interesting that you mention that. Georgina's brother Bob and one of Herbert's brothers had safe civil service jobs, clerical jobs. You know, security and probably a pension at the end of it, and perhaps because Herbert's father had been this slightly – well he'd gone bankrupt several times – they moved house about nine times in their childhood and so they valued security and safety . . .

JMcC: It was a common thing when you had a father who was a bit rackety.

AP: Yes, that's right "my job might not be all that exciting but at least it's safe" and also, coming back to Rosaline, maybe the move towards the labour movement and even Sylvia was linked with the communist movement, that was just a step too far for her – particularly when Herbert was a Conservative and an active Conservative!

JMcC: And that was one of the big surprises you sprang on me because I had a picture of this progressive guy – maybe he was interested in design, because he was working for the London County Council, and I was wrong.

AP: Yes, and also I did know her [Georgina's] brother Don – not as well as her – he was, like most of the McCheyne men, he was easy-going, generous. He was a salesman actually. He had the gift of the gab and so I think there's a sort of family characteristic coming out there, but again I'm sure he would have been a Conservative voter as well, so maybe Sylvia was moving just too far away for Rosaline to cope with.

JMcC: I think also there was the way people got involved in the Federation which was the crisis the First World War pushed the East End into (1). Maybe she was just somebody who responded to seeing all the shortages, people becoming unemployed, women losing their husbands . . . Herbert was too old to go into the forces, wasn't he? Or was he eligible to join up?

AP: He was born in 1870 so he would have been 44 when war broke out . . . too old.

JMcC: And conscription didn't start until 1916 so he would definitely have been too old.

AP: Yes 46, but Bob would have become eligible but he wasn't called up, it seems. I don't know quite what his work was but Georgina just said "Oh, he . . . you know he was a civil servant". That could have been anything. He could have been a postman. I think it was something clerical, probably something safe and boring.

JMcC: Well, better than going out and getting slaughtered I suppose.

AP: I'm sure he wouldn't have volunteered but he could easily have been conscripted. My grandfather was, even though farming was a reserved occupation, but, unfortunately, there were four brothers and the father working on the farm, and it was a big farm. But, eventually, one of the brothers had to be called up, and it was him. He was lucky enough to survive, mainly because he caught pneumonia before his unit was drafted abroad. He wasn't conscripted until the end of the war (1). It suddenly escalated then and then suddenly it was all over. I think . . . suddenly it was all over.

I can imagine Rosaline feeling terribly sorry for the women around her; the Bryant and May factory wasn't far away (2). It was just across the road. And so thinking about the contrast between Mountnessing Hall and Fairfield Road with the Bryant and May factory and the railway bridge with trains going by all day about four doors away and the bus station . . .

JMcC: It would have been filthy, wouldn't it?

AP: Yes, dirty and noisy.

JMcC: And that's another thing – her house – it must have been a nightmare just keeping things relatively clean (1).

AP: Yes, I've never heard about any mention of having help in the house, but I think sometimes some lower-middle-class women sometimes got somebody in to help with the heavy washing, so that might have been a possibility. I'm sure Georgina and the others loved going out in the fresh air, where everything was clean and there was space for everything. And they seemed to lead quite a good social life, according to my grandmother's diaries nearly every day they were playing cards and whist, "so and so came over for tea and someone else to supper" and it was like open house so I can understand why Georgina loved it. I never heard whether Rosaline ever went. Herbert used to go. It was the sort of thing you sent your children to for a nice healthy holiday.

JMcC: Let's come back to something from earlier. In the East End they used to have these huge families. It wouldn't have been unusual to have fourteen children (2). Do you have any idea why she had a tiny family in comparison?

AP: What I find fascinating, intriguing was this huge gap between the first child and the second child and it was the same in Rosaline's family, she had a much older brother, Elias, then there was a gap of 12 years or maybe more. Then she had a sister maybe two years older than her, Rachel, and then there was Rosaline. There could have been stillbirths and miscarriages in between that we don't know about and then there seemed to be almost a repeat of that because Rosaline herself she had Bob a year, a year and a half after they were first married, the normal sort of time. And that was in 1896 and then Georgina was born in 1907, and then Don in 1910. So there was an eleven-year gap [between Georgina and Bob]. In the 1911 census, the one they filled in themselves, when she answered the question that asks about live births and living children, she put three births. So, if there were, there could have been still births in between. My mother thought there was some story about twins who died. There might have been stillborn twins but there's no record of that and Georgina herself she didn't have children until 14 years after she married, no, 12 years after she married, there was this long gap so I don't know if it is something medical or genetic or if it was a choice.

JMcC: I think that is interesting because people with education at that point were just starting to get access to planning their family – through writings and there were products – sponges and barriers – probably the same kind of things people are using now. It's highly speculative, but you might think that a couple, they were fairly educated with a husband who, although he was a member of the local Conservative Tory Party, he was sceptical of religion and that was, if you'll pardon the pun, one of the biggest barriers to people using contraception was the belief that children were born at the will of God and that children were a gift and a gift from God, so who were we to put anything in the way. And I did wonder if that only applied to Catholic families – but apparently it was all across the board, all religions.

AP: Well it's an interesting thing to speculate on but we just don't know. I know with Georgina it was choice but they didn't have children until... it was useful to have a child because it kept her husband in the country during the Second World War. He wasn't sent overseas but, in any case – they absolutely adored them – once they had children which they never thought they wanted, they absolutely adored them, so it was a good thing in the end. I mean it must have been sad at the end of Rosaline's life, because her beloved son, Bob, – I get the impression he was the golden boy of the family, the good looking one – he died. (1) They were very close. Rosaline always lived either with, or next door to one of her sons throughout her life and Bob died before she did. Then, a year later her only granddaughter died. My mother has a memory of her crying, and I said "well, why was she crying?", and she said it was Carol's funeral, the little girl's funeral. I feel sad that the end of her life was – Herbert had died many years beforehand – she was comfortable and looked after but it must have been sad for her.

JMcC: Yes, people did grow to a great old age but it was much more unusual then.

AP: Yes, she was 84, and she didn't have to go into hospital or anything. I think Georgina was not far away and her surviving son lived next door. Yes, so she was looked after which was good.

JMcC: It's interesting, and I think the family story's interesting as well, because so many people in the East End they gradually worked their way out towards Essex. Can you describe their...

AP: Yes in 1925 they moved out into Leytonstone to Forest Drive. I don't know Forest Drive that well. They moved out there which was a little bit more leafy I think then and then that's when they went on the trip to Hainault Forest – you saw the photo. And then ten years later, by 1936, I think they had moved to Bridge Road in Upminster, a bit further out on the tube (2).

JMcC: That really fascinated me because my family moved out to a road that was practically parallel to that road. I had no idea when I found out that this was where she ended up. My family's path out along the District Line was very similar.

AP: Yes and Georgina, she married and settled not far away in Romford, Collier Row, Romford so she wasn't too distant. They always stayed close to each other. It's the gradual suburbanisation, isn't it, of the East End? I think it's still happening.

JMcC: Oh absolutely. So, what do you think was the most interesting part of Rosaline's story from your point of view? What have you come across that . . ?

AP: Oh that she was so deeply involved with the suffragettes. I got the impression from Georgina's story that she just went along out of curiosity to see what was going on – so the fact that she was so deeply involved I found that very interesting – and this intriguing thing about the resignation – I find that absolutely fascinating and it sort of spurred me on to research other members of her family more thoroughly. Another aspect is that one of her sisters-in-law, one of Herbert's sisters married a German national and I thought – well, how did they feel about that during the First World war? And you know all these aspects bubble up once you start researching.

JMcC: Yes, there was a lot of anti-German feeling around in the East End.

AP: There was, and yet the Germans were woven into the population. Quite thoroughly but he didn't seem to have any problems at all. He was . . . he had the vote which I was surprised at despite not being a British subject. He was in bakery, he used to work in the bakery industry. I think a lot of Germans were in bakeries and confectionery.

So, it sort of encouraged me to research the others further and to see what kind of contact there was between them.

JMcC: Is there a difference in the way you viewed Rosaline – from what you heard from Georgina to where you are now after doing some research?

AP: Oh yes, she's got much more depth and interest to her than I realised. I thought she was a typical stay-at-home, slightly genteel domestic lady who did all the right things – so nice clothes and played the piano and taught Georgina to be the same, like a little lady, but she was obviously a real thinker and activist which surprised me but I'm quite proud of her!

JMcC: Well I think what you've done, and to use a cliché, the journey you've been on, it's something I think that would be quite inspiring for other people to go on and start looking at their family and see what turns up and how their views alter as yours did.

AP: Oh absolutely. Well I was lucky that you'd done a lot of the research first and that's the thing if you can share with other people and come at it from different angles then you can get a much more rounded picture and discover your ancestors are more interesting than you thought originally.

JMcC: Thank you very much indeed, Anne, for taking the trouble to come all the way from Essex today and talk to me about Rosaline.

AP: It's a pleasure.

Rosaline McCheyne, Activist and Member of the East London Federation of Suffragettes, 1913-1916: Commentary on an Interview with her Descendant, Anne Padfield Recorded in October 2018

PAGE 8

Note 1 "JMcC: Hello Anne, I'm Jane McChrystal, project volunteer with the Women's Hall Exhibition interviewing you about your ancestor Rosaline McCheyne, member of the East London Federation of Suffragettes."

The Tower Hamlets Local History Library and Archive hosted a reimagining of the Women's Hall at 400 Old Ford Road in 2018 as part of the centenary celebrations of the Representation of the People Act, which granted the vote for the first time to women over the age of 30 with a property qualification.

The Women's Hall was the headquarters of the East London Federation of Suffragettes (ELFS) which was founded by Sylvia Pankhurst in 1914 after the

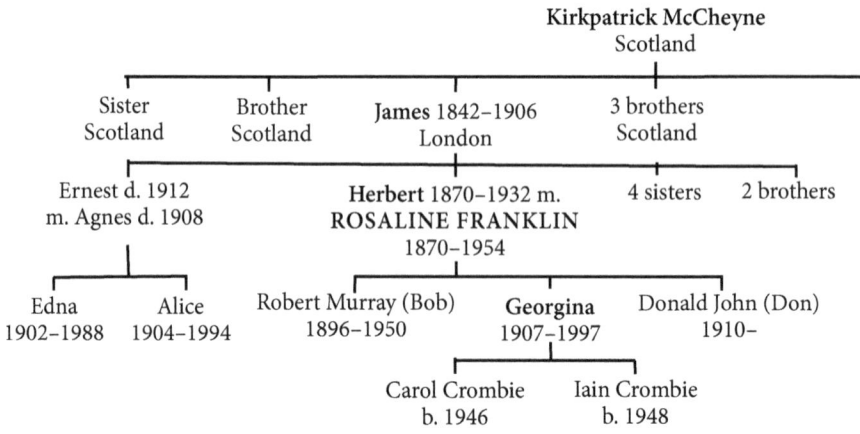

McCHEYNE FAMILY TREE (part)

split from the Women's Social and Political Union (WSPU), the mainstream movement led by Sylvia's mother, Emmeline and her sister, Christabel.

ELFS was active between 1914 to 1916 and the exhibition was designed to tell the story of its splendid achievements which, so far, have gone largely unrecognised. As well as campaigning for women's suffrage, the members of ELFS launched a programme to relieve the privations inflicted by the outbreak of the First World War on the people of the East End. They provided milk for hungry babies from a network of distribution centres and medical care for children in free clinics. Adults were given nourishing meals at their cost-price restaurants. They set up a toy factory where women worked in decent conditions for fair pay. A nursery run along Montessori lines took care of their children while they worked.

The exhibition highlighted heroic women such as Melvina Walker, Annie Barnes and Nellie Cressall who went on to change the lives of East Enders through their work as local borough councillors.

Note 2 "JMcC: You've already mentioned that you're related to Rosaline – perhaps you could say how."

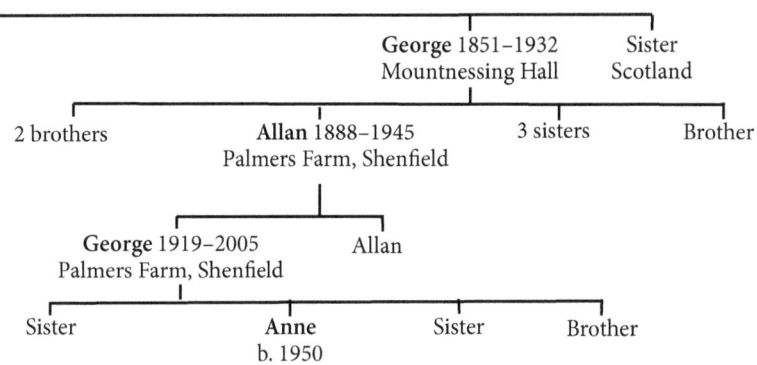

Herbert and my grandfather Allan were first cousins.
Ernest's and Herbert's children regularly visited Mountnessing Hall.
Georgina and her family regularly visited Palmers Farm.

COMMENTARY ON AN INTERVIEW WITH ANNE PADFIELD

PAGE 9

Note 1 "AP: *Before she [Georgina] had children, she worked as a lecturer at a technical college (1^a) in Dagenham (1^b).*"

Note 1^a It's possible that Georgina taught at the college in Longbridge Road, built in Dagenham in 1936 as one of four Essex regional technical colleges.

Their establishment marked a high point in the history of technical education in England. Earlier attempts in the twentieth century to create an effective system were undermined by the economic depression of the '20s and '30s.

There was another obstacle to providing government funding for a coherent system of technical education, the rather short-sighted, national view that supporting academic education was always more worthwhile than training students to a high level of technical competence. Then, as now, commentators deplored the scarcity of engineering skills in the workforce and the inferiority of the English technical education system in comparison to other countries such as Germany, which has a long history of combining vocational experience with secondary education.

The system Georgina worked in was an incoherent mix of day and evening classes provided by a variety of institutions, some with their origins in nineteenth century Mechanics' Institutes and the Working Men's Colleges. It was a muddle, but it did work for some people. A man who wanted to make a better life for his family could work and study at the same time for qualifications in technical subjects at low cost and increase his chances of getting a better job with higher wages.

Specialist training for lecturing in Technical Education did not appear until 1946, when Garnett College opened in South West London, so Georgina probably qualified for her post through becoming a skilled pattern-maker and showing an interest in teaching others.

For a comprehensive account of the history of technical education in England please see **Technical Education Matters** *website*

technicaleducationmatters.org
run by Richard Evans FInst.P. FCGI. FInst.I.M. CompCIPHE.

Note 1^b "*Dagenham*"

As part of the solution to London's early twentieth-century housing crisis, the London County Council got together with county councils outside the city to build new estates for Londoners stuck in the insanitary, overcrowded terraces and tenements left behind by Victorian slum landlords. One of these developments was the Becontree Estate in Dagenham completed in 1935:

. . . a London County Council scheme to build 29,000 new homes for some 145,000 London residents. Of those, 24,000 houses were to be built on 3,000 acres of market gardens, cottages and country lanes beyond London's eastern borders in Essex. municipaldreams.wordpress.com/2013/01/08/the-becontree-estate-built-in-england-where-the-most-revolutionary-social-changes-can-take-place-and-people-in-general-do-not-realise-that-they-have-occurred/

Only the most respectable of East Londoners were selected to move to the estate and later generations of architectural commentators have derided the uniformity of its streets and houses and a lack of amenities. But for the new arrivals, fresh air, green spaces, houses with indoor plumbing and separate bedrooms for children to sleep in made it "heaven with the gates off".

Georgina's students would no doubt have included women and girls from the Becontree Estate who had been moved out of the East End as part of the LCC's slum clearance programme. As a relatively prosperous family, who had decent accommodation in Fairfield Road, Bow, they would have initiated their own eastward journey and their route will be traced later on page 56 of this commentary.

PAGE 10

Note 1 "AP: . . . *and then during the Second World War there was the Make Do and Mend Policy – and she [Georgina] taught how to turn an old coat into a waistcoat or a pair of slippers or something . . ."*

Make do and mend was just one of many chirpy slogans broadcast by the government to keep the nation united in support of a state of total war. **Make do and mend** was coined by the Board of Trade in 1942 a year after the introduction of rationing of clothes and textiles.

The rationing scheme was intended to ensure the fair distribution of a limited clothing supply through the use of a coupon system, which could be subverted easily enough by anyone with money to spend on the black market and the aid of the spivs who operated it. Everyone else had to manage as best they could.

The Board of Trade encouraged them to mend worn garments or cut up those which were too far gone to be refashioned into smaller items of clothing. It produced books, leaflets and animations to get their message across and even produced their own poster girl in the form of a cartoon character, "Mrs. Sew and Sew". It instructed the people on how to sew on a patch, darn neatly and destroy clothes moths.

The Women's Voluntary Service did their bit by organising exchanges of clothes children had outgrown and holding knitting parties for the production of "comforts" for the troops, such as gloves and scarves.

No silks or satins were available, so some enterprising women made wedding dresses out of parachute silk left over from the First World War. The rest married in a two-piece skirt suit or "costume", as it was known, with matching hat.

Clothes rationing finally ended four years after the end of the Second World War in 1949.

The Imperial War Museum has further information on the policy posted at:
https://www.iwm.org.uk/history/10-top-tips-for-winning-at-make-do-and-mend

The BFI has a real curiosity in its archives "In Which We Live Being the Story of a Suit Told by Itself", a Public Information film made to promote **Make do and Mend** *in 1944 by Richard Massingham. It charts the progress of a suit* *from its own point of view, as its owner, John, goes from bachelorhood and on to marriage, fatherhood until he is called up and asks his wife to turn it into a pair of shorts and a skirt for his son and daughter, as he no longer has any use for it, as he'll be in uniform for the foreseeable future.*

You can find it at: player.bfi.org.uk/free/film/watch-in-which-we-live-being-the-story-of-a-suit-told-by-itself-1944-online

Note 2 "AP: . . . *but she was quite selective about what she said about her background. Because although she [Georgina] was technically a cockney, I suppose, she was born in Bow, she always said she lived in London."*

What did Anne mean when she said Georgina was technically a cockney?

For most people today, the cockney voice is probably typified by the Canning Town-born actor Danny Dyer in his role as Mick Carter of the long-running soap 'East Enders' and, like him, Georgina was born within the sound of the bells of St. Mary-le-Bow, Cheapside, which qualified her as a cockney. But, as Anne told me after our interview, Georgina spoke English with received pronunciation, the standard mode of the middle classes, rather than adopting the accent of her fellow East Enders.

She seemed distant in other ways too from her childhood neighbours in her enthusiastic pursuit of music, drawing and literature, which Anne mentions in other parts of the interview. She was also vague about exactly where she came from in London.

For anyone trying to make their way in the world in the years before the Second World War, "speaking nicely", taking an interest in the arts, and coming from an unspecified part of London would have brought notable advantages denied to the seemingly less refined individual.

People whose cultural identity is tied to regions of social and economic deprivation, as we know, are frequently looked down upon and denied opportunities, a tendency which was even stronger when Georgina was growing up. Dropping an aitch or open acknowledgement of growing up in the East End could have attracted contempt from others and hindered her ability to get on in life.

Being a cockney brought its own particular problems. Cockneys had a negative image traceable to nineteenth-century street markets like Spitalfields and Petticoat lane, where the traders or costermongers, were notorious for sharp practice – displaying the good fruit and vegetables on the front of the barrow and slipping the bad ones from the middle into the customer's bag. Too poor to bother with conforming to social norms like marriage, they were seen as immoral as well as dishonest. Their flash clothes and ready patter inspired mistrust in East London and beyond. During the twentieth century the image evolved into that of the "barrow boy", a derogatory label for bright lads from the East End who went to work on the trading floors of the nearby City of London banks and the Stock Exchange.

Since the Second World War as East Londoners moved out along the District Line and advanced into Essex, taking their dialect with them, new generations of Bangladeshi and Somali immigrants arrived and created a new linguistic culture dubbed "Multi-cultural London English" by the experts. The sound of the bells of St. Mary-le-Bow has been drowned out by the noise of traffic and London cockneys recede into a folkloric past. Their voice can still be heard every day on the streets and buses of East London, usually among some of the more elderly members of the population.

Detailed descriptions of the lives, conditions and nature of the costermongers can be found in Henry Mayhew's **London Labour and the London Poor,** *a piece of journalism which appeared in the 1840s in the Morning Chronicle and later compiled in book form.*

A more recent edition was published in Penguin Classics in 1985.

PAGE 11

Note 1 "**AP:** *And she said she went to a demonstration once where Sylvia*

Pankhurst was addressing people and it was broken up by the police. But she wasn't too involved in it. She made it sound more like she was on the sidelines . . ."

This was the May Day Procession in 1914 which ended in a rally in Hackney's Victoria Park on Sunday, 24th May. In fact, Rosaline played an important role in the action of the day. She held ELFS' funds which she used to bail out members and supporters who were arrested and taken to Bow Police station. You can find out more in articles 7 and 6, pages 73-77: **May Day Procession** and **A Day in the Life of an Activist**.

Later in the interview Anne mentions that even Rosaline's grandson, Iain, didn't seem to know about her particular contribution to this historic event.

PAGE 12

Note 1 "AP: . . . her best friends and contacts were our side of the family and the descendants of those at Mountnessing Hall, that was her social circle . . . "

Here are Anne's family memories of the McCheynes at Mountnessing Hall written in her own words:

Mountnessing Hall was a favourite place for the 'London McCheynes' to visit after Herbert's uncle George McCheyne settled there as a tenant farmer in about 1900. Scottish-born farmers were famously good at networking, especially with their relations, and regular visits and letters were the norm. Besides, London was a dirty city at that time, and Herbert and Rosaline's Fairfield Road home in Bow was near the railway, with a factory in one direction and a motor-bus station in the other. Edwardian doctors prescribed lashings of fresh air for every ailment, and fear of TB in particular led parents to send their children to stay with country cousins as often as they could.

The McCheynes' terraced house was two-up and two-down with a basement. Although there were always five or six of them living there, it was considered a comfortable size for a lower-middle-class town home, and many identical houses in the same road housed up to thirteen occupants. Mountnessing Hall, by contrast, was a large impressive farmhouse, with 17 rooms and unlimited fresh air. It was next to St Giles' Church but a good mile or more from the main village of Mountnessing, which was strung out along the former Roman Road. This was a common pattern in Essex, where the historic chief manor house and church, with a few scattered cottages, stood isolated from the rest of the settlement.

Shenfield station, though, was less than three miles away and, with a fast train service from Liverpool Street and a pony and trap from the station, the East End family could go from Bow to Mountnessing Hall in about an hour and a half. Rosaline's children Bob, Georgina and Don were regular visitors, as well as their cousins Edna and Alice McCheyne, and probably other London cousins too. George and Annie's family were all quite a bit older than the London youngsters, apart from Rosaline's eldest son Bob, who was almost of their generation. He was apparently in love with his cousin Mary McCheyne – she had lots of admirers – but as a modest London clerk, he wouldn't have been considered a good match. She married, as would be expected, a neighbouring Scottish farmer's son, and Bob eventually married a London girl.

The visitors' first view as they approached Mountnessing Hall would have been the spire of St. Giles' Church, then the impressive brick frontage of the house as they drove past a courtyard of farm buildings. Until the twenty-first century it was thickly covered in ivy. Sharp-eyed visitors might have noticed that the "window" above the central front door was a blank recess, painted to match the other windows. Although it looks like a symmetrical brick house from the front, behind the façade is a sixteenth- or seventeenth-century timber-framed house with a typically irregular layout inside. Plenty of alterations had been made over the years: in the eighteenth century the roof was re-aligned and the brick façade added, and in the nineteenth century a whole new range was added along the back.

The most striking feature for any visitor was that the entrance hall was huge – much bigger than any of the other rooms. George and Annie's leather-bound Family Bible was on display there on a table. They had written in the details of their marriage in Scotland, then the names of all their children and their dates of birth as the family grew, and sadly recorded the death of one daughter at the age of seven. (Older daughter Annie later scratched out all the dates of birth when she became sensitive about people knowing her age!)

Because of the extra thickness of the front wall, several of the south-facing windows had panelled window-seats. As an avid reader, Georgina at least would have loved to sit there in the sunshine with a favourite book. By the time she was old enough to visit, the eldest son Andrew had married and moved to a farm in Wickford. The others, however, were all still at home in 1911 and working at Mountnessing Hall. *"Farmer's daughter"* was recorded as the girls' occupation because they had to help with the dairying (Annie went to Writtle Institute to learn butter- and cheese-making) and in the fields at busy times. David, the youngest, was still at school at 15 but no doubt had to pull his weight once he got home.

The First World War cast its shadow over many lives, but farmers were in a protected occupation and not so badly affected, apart from many of their horses being requisitioned and some of their farmworkers volunteering. When conscription was later introduced, a family with four healthy sons, three of them unmarried, had to justify not joining up. At a tribunal in Romford in May 1917, the chairman reluctantly allowed them all to continue working at home for the time being but urged them to find substitutes quickly so they could serve. Surely a family of this standing would want to have at least one representative in the Army? "Wars may come and wars may go, but this farm goes on for ever" appeared to be the McCheyne motto', he drily commented when faced with their obvious lack of enthusiasm. (Eventually in June 1918, son Allan was called up. He did his training, but caught pneumonia just in time to avoid going to France.)

Despite the war, social life in the countryside continued: the 1917 and 1918 diaries of Betsy Hodge, a farmer's daughter from nearby Buttsbury who married Allan, record frequent visits to Mountnessing Hall for teas, parlour games, and whist drives in the village hall. 'Coz Bob' is mentioned several times, and a visit by 'little Georgie'. The girls went shopping together in London and saw a show. They were little affected by food rationing, introduced towards the end of the war, as the farm had plenty of eggs, milk, butter and cheese, as well as the pigeons, pheasants, partridges and rabbits that the boys shot.

By 1923, George's wife Annie had died and the rest of the family had married and moved out, leaving George alone in the big house. Eventually eldest son Andrew and his formidable wife Bella moved in and took over the tenancy of the farm until Andrew's death in 1944. A new tenant took over and McCheynes at Mountnessing Hall were a thing of the past.

PAGE 13

Note 1 "AP: *She often mentioned he was a teacher but it was quite difficult to prise out of her the fact that he was a woodwork teacher.*"

Herbert McCheyne's position as a woodwork instructor, recorded in the Census of 1911, would have made a significant contribution to Rosaline's capacity for work as an ELFS activist.

The majority of East End women had husbands who were employed on a casual basis. They worked in the London Docks and factories when work was available and were laid off when it wasn't. To fill in the gaps the women might have taken in washing, gone out cleaning or taken on piece work, as well as looking after large families and their own homes. Many simply would not have had time to give to campaigning for ELFS.

Herbert's earlier occupation, as a pattern maker, was a highly skilled one, which involved making wooden models for metal machine parts. He was able to use his skills developed in that job to move into a position as a teacher with the technical panel of the London County Council. His steady wage meant Rosaline did not have to take up poorly-paid exhausting labour and left her with time to dedicate to ELFS.

PAGE 14

Note 1 "AP: Yes, there were some photos taken in the '20s when Georgina she would have been in her early twenties and that's the only photograph that I have of Rosaline herself, but unfortunately she's wearing a great heavy fur, and she's wearing one of those cloche hats, so you can barely see, she's wearing glasses and apart from that you can't . . ."

Rosaline, Georgina, her friend, Doris Thompson and Herbert

Anne told me later that the photos were taken in Hainault Forest in 1928. You can see how smartly the McCheynes had dressed for their trip to the forest which was about 10 miles from their home in Forest Drive, Leytonstone where they had moved in 1925. Their relaxed pose suggests that the photos were taken by someone who went on the trip with them, possibly Bob or Don.

They had clearly become caught up in the popular enthusiasm for photography, sparked in 1898 by the invention of the Kodak Box Brownie. By the time this photograph was taken the Box Brownie 2 was in production, a simple, inexpensive camera affordable to most people. People simply loaded the film, focused on the image they wanted to capture through the viewfinder, and clicked the shutter to take their picture. Then, they sent the film off for development. This process guaranteed Kodak a never-ending stream of customers for their products.

The Box Brownie 2 was in production until 1936 and its sturdy, uncomplicated construction ensured that many are still around today. Their widespread use during the twentieth century has left us with a rich legacy of photos documenting people like the McCheynes relaxing during their time away from work. The family were on the up: they had a smarter address, leisure and money to spare for a nice trip, and good quality clothing to pose in for their photographs.

PAGE 15

Note 1 "AP: *Yes, oh absolutely, but it meant you could see very little of her [Rosaline's face], but the photograph you showed me, I found here in the Dreadnought, her photograph as a committee member, and I found that very interesting. She has the same high cheek bones as Georgina and also she was sort of not looking straight at the camera, a bit uncomfortable about being photographed – a bit like Georgina, who would often slightly turn away.*

Perhaps that's my imagination but I thought I could see that in Rosaline as well. It sort of fits with her not pushing herself forward as well. She'd rather be useful in the background than be up front."

Note 2 *"JMcC: Of course, we both know she played a part in every aspect of the work of the Federation".*

A report in the *Woman's Dreadnought* of 24th July 1915 carries a farewell to Rosaline as she moves out of the area. It thanks her for her involvement in every aspect of ELFS' activities. You can find out more about the role she played in **"She Carried on in the most Splendid Way"**, which appears as Article 1 on pages 57-60.

PAGE 16

Note 1 *"AP: Sylvia Pankhurst didn't have to think about housework or family responsibilities so she could probably organise things without having to take those things into account".*

Sylvia arrived in the East End of London in 1912 to support George Lansbury's campaign for election as a Labour MP on the "Votes for Women" ticket. It failed, but Sylvia stayed and set up a branch of the Women's Social and Political Union there with her companions Norah Smyth and Zelie Emerson.

Sylvia's faith in the potential of the impoverished women of the East End was at the root of her split from the WSPU and the mainstream women's suffrage movement. Her sister, Christabel, believed that only the best-educated and most vigorous women were fit to fight for the right to vote and the women of the East End did not qualify – they had scarcely any education and were worn out with raising enormous families and hard work. According to Sylvia, working-class women had to play a part in the fight for women's suffrage, as they were integral to a broader struggle for social justice and economic equality for all. Consequently, she left the WSPU, set up the East London Federation of Suffragettes in 1914 and established their headquarters at 400 Old Ford Road.

As Anne remarked, Sylvia would not have been over-burdened with domestic duties. She was ably supported by Norah Smyth who provided funds and managed daily affairs on her behalf. Plenty of other people in the area came to her aid, including Jessica Payne and her husband who took care of her in their home on 28 Old Ford Road when she was recovering from her hunger strike on release from Holloway Prison in 1913.

Sylvia came from a prosperous, middle-class background and was educated to a high level at Manchester Grammar School and the Royal College of Art. As a result, she was free from the necessity to marry, submit to a husband's authority and run a household for him. Even so, the degree of courage she showed in her defiance of the established order, a quality shared with her mother and sisters, mark her out as an exceptional individual.

The desire to achieve social justice for all, which drove her throughout her life, was the inheritance from her father Richard, a campaigning barrister, who died in 1897, when she was 15 years old. She committed to the cause of socialism after the Russian Revolution, but split from the British Communist movement in the '20s. The rest of her life was devoted to the causes of anti-fascism and anti-colonialism and in particular the people of Ethiopia where she went to live in 1956. Her dedication to them was recognised in 1960 when she died and was honoured with a state funeral. She is buried in Addis Ababa.

She was survived by her son Richard, scholar and champion of the Ethiopian people and father of Helen Pankhurst who carries on the family tradition as an international campaigner for women's rights to this day.

Sarah Jackson's book tells more of Sylvia's story and other extraordinary women of ELFS.

Note 2 "AP: Before marriage she [Rosaline] was a post office sorting clerk. I think that was quite a respected job and you would have had to be well-organised and quite meticulous to do that, so that would have stood her in quite good stead for the admin and that kind of thing she did for the Federation."

Rosaline's job as a sorting clerk, a "brain worker", before marriage distinguished her from many of the young women in her neighbourhood who were destined for the sweatshops and factories of the East, where they would have laboured long hours for pitiful wages in dangerous conditions.

Rosaline must have benefited from an enormous expansion in the provision of secondary education which resulted from the Education Act of 1870. The Act would have opened up the opportunity to stay at school beyond the age of thirteen and develop the more advanced skills in literacy and numeracy needed to equip her for a clerical position, a kind of education neatly tailored to meet the needs of employers.

Rosaline was also part of a new wave of women being recruited at the end of the nineteenth century to replace men in the lower ranks of clerical workers, where they undertook the more tedious and repetitive tasks at a lower rate of pay.

While it would have been difficult for Rosaline to enter a private, commercial enterprise at this time without useful family contacts, which she lacked in her social position, there were no such barriers to finding employment with the Post Office or Civil Service. As soon as she married, she would have been compelled to give up her occupation, a practice which persisted well into the twentieth century.

Michael Heller's thesis "London clerical workers 1880 –1914: the Search for Stability" is a detailed study of the background to the environment Rosaline worked in. U602595%20redacted.PDF

PAGE 18

Note 1 *"JMcC: Actually, that was quite an important trend about that period. Women were able to start going out and about on the street and travel without being thought about as "low"."*

Rosaline's house was on the same street as the Bow Bus Garage, built in 1908, which stands there to this day. It is still the starting point of the Number 8 bus and must have given East Enders improved access to shops, entertainments and new opportunities for employment in the West End, as well as providing a boon to women who were gaining new freedoms in the social sphere at the time.

You can read about the changing circumstances of women's lives in Article 3, pages 63-66: **The Street Where She Lived**

Note 2 *"Who Do You Think You are Magazine"*

This is published monthly by the BBC to help people to discover their family history and accompany the TV series of the same name.

http://www.whodoyouthinkyouaremagazine.com

Note 3 *"So I looked up "Mrs. McCheyne" in the Newspaper Archive ..."*

The National Newspaper Archive is an invaluable resource for anyone investigating their family history

http://www.nationalarchives.gov.uk/help-with-your-research/research-guides/newspapers/

PAGE 19

Note 1 *"JMcC: I think it's very interesting you were saying Georgina was always saying "oh Father was a teacher" but nowadays we just go and look at something like Ancestry.com and we know exactly what Herbert was."*

Herbert's occupation was revealed in the 1911 Census recorded online in Ancestry.com, another important resource for family historians. Some local authority library services provide access to it for their users. Individuals can take out their own subscription.

PAGE 20

*Note 1 "AP: **Sadly, both their [Herbert's nieces] parents died – one in 1908 and then one in 1912. They were basically – they were orphaned in 1912. At that time I think Don, he was one or two, and Georgina was five, and I'm quite surprised the children ended up in a children's home and I thought well that's strange they only lived a few streets away. Why didn't Rosaline take them in? Particularly as in her own family, her parents adopted a much younger child [Minnie Curtis], presumably from difficult circumstances or from a relative – it [adoption] wasn't formal then".*

When Herbert's nieces, Alice and Edna, were orphaned in 1912 there was, as Anne observed, no formal adoption process. She also mentioned that Rosaline's parents, the Franklins, took a child, Minnie Curtis, into their home and brought her up as one of their own, a very common practice.

For many children, informal adoption was the best solution for those who were born illegitimate, had lost their parents or whose parents could not afford to bring them up. However, the lack of regulation of the process opened up other children in these sad circumstances to physical and emotional abuse and even death.

Some people who took in unwanted children were looking for cheap labour on a farm or in the home. Others were handed into the care of "baby farmers", often a last resort for unmarried women who gave birth to a child. Typically, a woman in this position worked in domestic service and handed over part of her wages or a lump sum to a woman who promised to take care of the baby in return.

Such an arrangement was wide open to exploitation. There was no limit to the number of children a woman might take or supervision of the quality of care she offered them. Mothers who worked long hours, had few holidays and scarce resources were in no position to check on the welfare of the children they handed over to another's care.

A number of scandals broke out in the nineteenth century, the worst of which concerned Amelia Dyer who was hanged in 1896 for the murder of Doris Marmon, the daughter of a barmaid, who had been entrusted to her. When Doris's case was investigated, further murders were discovered and it was estimated that in the end she was responsible for the deaths of more than 400 babies and children.

Amelia Dyer's trial and execution might well have provided the popular press with acres of sensationalist material about an individual, evil child murderer, but it exposed something very wrong with the English legal and medical systems and the wider society they operated in. Amelia Dyer was known to have a history of mental health problems and had spent time in a number of psychiatric hospitals. In 1879 she was imprisoned for allowing children to die of neglect and yet she remained free to accept money from desperate mothers for years after her release.

Every time she was at risk of exposure she simply moved on. It seems that the lives of the most unfortunate children in Victorian England were of so little value that no one bothered about their disappearance or the perpetrators.

In response to the scandal the local administrators of the Poor Law and charitable institutions started schemes for boarding out children from orphanages and workhouses with families. Finally, the government passed the Adoption Act in 1926 making it compulsory to assess the suitability of prospective adoptive parents and register an adoption in exactly the same way as the birth of a child.

You can find out more in:

Montgomery, Heather (2010). Unwanted children and adoption in England. In: Brockliss, Laurence and Montgomery, Heather eds. 'Childhood and Violence in the Western Tradition'. *Childhood in Archaeology* Monograph (1). Oxford, U.K.: Oxbow Books.

PAGE 24

Note 1 "AP: I think she [Sylvia Pankhurst[was pushing them [ELFS] to do more and more, maybe it was the chalking – was that writing slogans? There was a lot of chalking, yes, because they would have to buy chalk and she's saying, you know, "you must"...

Chalking the pavement was a popular way of broadcasting messages about the cause used both by the WSPU and ELFS. Two or three suffragettes would get together to write slogans or announce the time and venues of meetings on the pavement in green, purple and white chalks, attracting others in the immediate area to work out the message that would result from their work. It was an effective way to promote the cause and less risky, say, than smashing windows, as there was only one arrest ever recorded for this form of activism.

Note 2 "JMcC: I think you've picked up on something because the Federation turned into a part of the labour movement in the end, part of the growing Labour Party, and obviously, round here with the docks, trade unionism was born in places like the East End and there was the first dockers' strike here."

The ELFS name changed to Worker's Suffrage Federation in 1916 and former ELFS' members, such as the Cohen sisters, went on to take up the communist cause, fired up by the 1917 Russian Revolution. Others became committed to pacifism and ending the First World War.

In 1916 the Speaker's Conference was convened to determine who would be given the vote as it had proved impossible for the House of Commons to reach agreement. In 1917 the Conference proposed that women over 30 who were graduates, property owners or tenant householders would be eligible, criteria which would become law in the Representation of the People Act in 1918.

PAGE 25

Note 1 "JMcC: I think also there was the way people got involved in the Federation which was the crisis the First World War pushed the East End into."

Within days of the outbreak of World War One the East End was hit by food shortages and layoffs. Men volunteered for military service leaving the women and children to wait at home for a government separation allowance. The allowance was meagre, took a long time to come through and was withdrawn if the recipient was suspected of starting a relationship with another man. Life in the East End was already precarious and war inflicted even greater privations on the population.

ELFS took immediate practical action.

They set up cost price restaurants around the East End to provide highly calorific meals suitable for people who did hard physical work. Some of the food was donated by local people and vegetables were supplied from the vegetable patch cultivated at the back of the Women's Hall.

No one was turned away, even if they couldn't afford tuppence for a meal, and a ticketing system ensured that diners didn't know whether the person sitting next to them had paid for their dinner or not, an arrangement consistent with the ELFS conviction that all should be equal.

If adults struggled to gain adequate nourishment during the war, mothers were even more hard pressed to feed their babies and children and ELFS responded by setting up milk distribution centres. It soon became apparent that malnourished babies could find it difficult to keep down their milk and mothers needed instruction in special feeding techniques.

Medical professionals were brought in to help them and soon they were also offering free treatment from a network of clinics, the first of which was set up in 1915 on the site of a pub, the Gunmaker's Arms on Old Ford Road and renamed the Mother's Arms.

They set up a toy factory at 45 Norman Road. The factory filled a gap in the market created by the war, as most toys had previously been imported from Germany, but it was also established to provide an alternative to the appalling conditions of labour endured by women of the East End in their homes and factories. The women earned decent wages for reasonable hours of work in a safe environment. They produced high quality goods which were put on sale in West End department stores.

For 3d a day mothers who worked at the ELFS' toy factory could leave their children in the care of the nursery, which was one of the first in England to employ the educational methods of Maria Montessori, pioneered with the street children of Naples.

After the First World War ended ex-members of ELFS, like Nellie Cressall, continued the work the Federation had begun. She went on to become a prominent local government politician and survived into the 1960s to see East Londoners' lives transformed by the creation of the National Health Service, a system of welfare benefits and the availability of decent social housing. It must have seemed ELFS' vision of social equality and justice for all was about to come true.

PAGE 26

Note 1 *"I'm sure he [Rosaline's son, Bob] wouldn't have volunteered [to serve in the armed forces during the First World War] but he could easily have been conscripted. My grandfather was, even though farming was a reserved occupation, but, unfortunately there were four brothers and the father working on the farm, and it was a big farm. But eventually, one of the brothers had to be called up, and it was him. He was lucky enough to survive, mainly* because he caught pneumonia before his unit was drafted abroad. He wasn't conscripted until the very end of the war" (1).

Compulsory service in the armed services during the First World War was introduced in 1916. The Military Service Act enforced military service for all men between the ages of 18 and 41, when men were volunteering in insufficient numbers to continue supporting the war effort.

Certain exemptions were made in the form of "reserved" or "scheduled" occupations, such as farmers, doctors, teachers, clergymen, coal miners and those engaged in any industry involved in the manufacture of arms. It can only be assumed that Bob's occupation was included in the schedule as he doesn't seem, as far as we know, to have suffered from any illness or disability that would have prevented him from joining up.

Tower Hamlets Local History Library and Archive holds the records of the Poplar Military Service Tribunal where the details of every appeal made against conscription were logged between 1916-1918.

Note 2 "I can imagine Rosaline feeling terribly sorry for the women around her; the Bryant and May factory wasn't far away."

The Match Girls' strike took place in 1888 in the factory on Fairfield Road where Rosaline would later make her home. You can find out more about the strike and the radical tradition in the East End of London which were part of Rosaline's inheritance in Article 2, pages 61-62.

PAGE 27

Note 1 "JMcC: It [Fairfield Road] would have been filthy, wouldn't it?

AP: Yes, dirty and noisy.

JMcC: And that's another thing – her house – it must have been a nightmare just keeping things relatively clean."

Article 5, pages 70-72, **"On the Home Front with Rosaline"** describes the kind of domestic regime living in 55 Fairfield Road would have imposed on Rosaline.

Note 2 JMcC: *Let's come back to something from earlier. In the East End they used to have these huge families. It wouldn't have been unusual to have fourteen children.*

In our interview Anne wonders whether Rosaline's small family was linked with patterns of fertility in the McCheyne family. In Article 4, pages 67-69, **Rosaline and Herbert**, I consider how a reasonably well-educated couple might have gone about planning a family in the early twentieth century. Herbert's sceptical approach to Christianity could also have fostered a positive attitude towards using contraception.

PAGE 29

Note 1 I mean it must have been sad at the end of Rosaline's life, because her beloved son, Bob, – I get the impression he was the golden boy of the family, the good looking one – he died.

Bob is in the back row standing second from the left.

Note 2 "*JMcC: . . . I think the family story's interesting as well, because so many people in the East End, they gradually worked their way out towards Essex. Can you describe their . . .*

AP: *Yes in 1925 they moved out into Leytonstone to Forest Drive. I don't know Forest Drive that well. They moved out there which was a little bit more leafy, I think, then and then that's when they went on the trip to Hainault Forest – you saw the photo. And then ten years later, by 1936, I think they had moved to Bridge Avenue in Upminster, a bit further out on the tube*".

The McCheynes' first move to Forest Drive was to a road of decent Victorian terraces in Leytonstone, close to the outskirts of Epping forest, but was still an East London address. Moving to Upminster would have represented a step up, a new address in suburbia.

The cockney exodus was made possible by the extension of the District Line to Upminster in 1932. Upminster would have looked positively rural to the migrating East Enders with its working windmill, the ancient Norman church of St. Laurence and proximity to the open countryside of Essex, even if their arrival meant burying the fields under the serried ranks of bay-fronted semis and bungalows which cover them now. A longish commute was the price of benefiting from the fresh air of a new garden suburb while keeping a foothold in the London employment market.

ARTICLE 1

She Carried on in the Most Splendid Way . . .

"Mrs. McCheyne and Mrs. Mantle have carried on in the most splendid way, the work of our Bromley Office and Baby Clinic at 53 St. Leonard's Street, ever since these were started. Now we regret to announce that Mrs. McCheyne is compelled to relinquish her work there as she is obliged to leave the district.

All the ELFS' members know Mrs. McCheyne, for she was one of our first recruits in East London, and has always been one of our hardest workers, having served on the ELFS Social Committees and in many other ways as well as Joint Honorary Secretary in Bromley.

We all thank her and hope that we shall see her from time to time."
Woman's Dreadnought, 24th July, 1915

Mrs. Rosaline McCheyne regularly attended meetings of the East London Federation of Suffragettes at Old Ford Road and Railway Street between February 2014 and February 2016, an exciting period in the history of the Federation, and the minutes of the meetings afford us occasional glimpses of the woman and the splendid work she did in the Bromley Office and elsewhere.

It's true that there are no records of her going on hunger strike or being arrested. She did not have the ear of the Prime Minister, H.H. Asquith, or the Leader of the Independent Labour Party, Kier Hardie, but as a member of ELFS she made a real difference to the lives of women and children of the East End. She is one of the many who worked tirelessly for women's suffrage but have all but disappeared from its history.

Her endeavours did not put her in the spotlight but they required hard work, dedication and courage. Canvassing and selling the *Woman's Dreadnought* on the streets of Bow was no easy job.

The minutes repeatedly document how difficult it could be to find a pitch for them and sales fluctuated. The minutes of 17th May reported that Rosaline was selling around 28 newspapers a week and, at one point around July 1915 sales in the Bromley district hit 1,000 a week. As Joint Honorary Secretary of the Bow district ELFS, Rosaline must have had a hand in this success by finding suitable pitches and recruiting and organising its sellers efficiently.

She does, however, report that collecting subscriptions was a tough call, which is hardly surprising, when many of the women she was trying to collect them from struggled to find enough money to feed and clothe their families.

Whether she was canvassing, recruiting or selling newspapers, her work on the streets must have required considerable self-confidence, as women had only recently gained the freedom to operate unaccompanied in the public sphere without being viewed as improper.

Not every East Ender was a supporter of the cause, and I'm fairly sure that Rosaline needed to combine an assertive manner, with the ability to convey that she didn't take herself too seriously in order to stake her place on the streets of East London. Then, as now, East Enders are ever alert to anyone who appears "up themselves" and will quickly let them know of their shortcomings.

Ten minutes' walk from Rosaline's home in Fairfield Road, the work she did with Mrs. Mantle at the Baby Clinic, 53 St. Leonard's Street was life-saving.

When World War One broke out in 1914, the price of food rocketed and racketeers profited from fears of shortages among the wealthy who were prepared to pay them even more. As a result, the poor inhabitants of East London could no longer buy the milk to feed their babies, which they had been scarcely able to afford before the war. Disgracefully, supplies of milk intended for the East End were diverted to the West End where, it was rumoured, they were fed to lap dogs.

The ELFS swung into action. Baby clinics and milk distribution centres were set up around the East End, including the clinic in St. Leonard's Street. Mothers brought their starving children to the clinic for milk and, if they were too sick to digest it, the ELFS workers advised them on methods of feeding. They also distributed virol*, barley and eggs. Free medical treatment was available and mothers were provided with feeding charts and health information leaflets.

Article 7, pages 77-78, Women's May Day, 24th May 1914 describes the dramatic events which occurred on 24th May 1914 in Victoria Park, where the Police violently broke up Sylvia Pankhurst's bodyguard to arrest her and take her off to Holloway Prison.

Rosaline may not have been in the vanguard of the procession from 400 Old Ford Road but, as the minutes of the 16th May show, she was on hand to arrange bail for any member of ELFS arrested that day.

Somehow this seems typical of the role Rosaline played in ELFS. Much of her work was essential but invisible. Acting as Joint Honorary Secre-

---

* A sweet, brown, sticky by-product of the brewing industry, high in nutrients, still available until the 1970s and much in demand from mothers anxious about their children's nutritional intake.

tary in the Bromley office and serving the ELFS Social Commitees required all those administrative skills; timetabling, record-keeping, co-ordinating and directing others and keeping them all informed, to create a mesh which holds an organisation together and enables it to run day to day. It is no wonder, then, that she received such a warm tribute in the *Dreadnought* on the announcement of her departure from ELFS.

The minutes show that Rosaline did return from time to time, and she is last mentioned on 21st February 1916. The traces of her life and work in the East End of London are still there for us to see in the *Dreadnought*, the Census of 1911 and the ELFS' archive.

If she lived until the age of 75, a not unreasonable expectation for a woman born in 1870, she would have witnessed the devastating consequences of economic depression in the 1930s and the Second World War. Both her sons became eligible for conscription, Robert in the First World War and Donald at the beginning of the Second. Georgina, at least, benefited from the struggles of the ELFS by getting the vote at the age of 21 in 1939.

It can only be hoped that she and her family survived to see the election of Clement Attlee's Labour Government in 1945 and the foundation of the welfare state, a system which would finally achieve many of the aspirations the ELFS worked so hard for among the people of the East End of London three decades before.

SOURCES

ELFS Committee Meeting Minutes between 28th February 1914 and 21st February 1916, transcribed by Rosemary Lucas

Harrison, S. *Sylvia Pankhurst: the Rebellious Suffragette*. Golden Guides Press 2012.

Jackson, S and Taylor, R. *Voices from History: East London Suffragettes*. The History Press 2014.

ARTICLE 2

Rosaline McCheyne: Coming of Age in the East End and a Radical Inheritance

In the late nineteenth century the East End of London was a crucible for radical ideas and activism fuelled by the years of brutal working conditions, poverty and appalling housing endured by the labouring classes. The potential to achieve lasting social and political change and improve the life of the people acted as a magnet to East London for philanthropists, religious non-conformists and revolutionaries from the rest of the country and Europe.

In 1888 a landmark in the history of labour took place in the Bryant and May factory, Bow, which surely must have had a lasting impression on the young Rosaline McCheyne who turned 18 that year.

The workforce of Bryant and May was composed largely of very young women who worked up to 14 hours a day for very low pay which was cut down by fines for misdemeanours such as going to the toilet without permission and talking. With the support of Annie Besant, and her flair for publicity, they went on strike for and won better wages, the abolition of fines and a separate space for eating.

This last was important because the women and girls worked in an atmosphere saturated with yellow phosphorous. This highly toxic substance causes phossy jaw, a horrific disease which destroys the sufferer's facial bones and ends in death. When the girls ate on the factory floor they not only inhaled the phosphorous but ingested it with their food.

After the strike, William Booth, founder of the Salvation Army, joined the women and girls to mount a successful campaign to force Bryant and May to substitute harmless red phosphorous for the deadly yellow variety in the manufacture of matches.

To witness these poorly-organised women and girls, with scant formal education, transform themselves into an effective force against the might of Bryant and May, must have been truly inspiring. 25 years after their victory, Rosaline signed up to the East London Federation of Suffragettes to become one of its most well-known, hard-working activists who "carried on in the most splendid way" on behalf of women in the East End.

55 Fairfield Road, Bow

SOURCE

Raw, L. *Striking a Light: the Bryant and May Matchwomen and their Place in History*. Continuum Press 2011.

ARTICLE 3

Rosaline McCheyne and the Street Where She Lived

Fairfield Road is fairly long, fairly wide and mostly residential, with a mix of Victorian terraces and low-rise private and social modern housing lining both sides.

Rosaline's three-storey terraced house, number 55, is still there, two doors up from a former pub, the Bromley Arms, and two minutes' walk from the imposing red-brick entrance to the fashionable Bow Quarter, site of the Bryant and May Factory until 1979.

Today it's a typical East End street: urban, but not gritty, with a steady flow of traffic linking the Bow Road at its south with Tredegar Road at its north.

We would have recognised Fairfield Road as it was in 1911 but, I think, Rosaline inhabited a livelier environment than the one we see today, where people did business, worked and socialised with each other, as well as making homes for themselves.

The Edwardian period was a time of enormous social change when the emergence of respectable middle- and upper-middle-class women into the public domain was made possible by new opportunities for philanthropic work, shopping and travelling by new forms of public transport.

It became perfectly acceptable for a woman to carry out these activities without a chaperone. Rosaline was well-placed to take advantage of these broadening horizons.

The construction of the Bow Bus Garage opposite number 55 in 1908 must have been a boon. With the new-found freedom to travel alone, she was able to take the motor buses, introduced to the transport system in 1902, to get to wherever she needed to fulfil her duties to ELFS, whether she was going to join a procession or attend a social committee meeting as Joint Honorary Secretary. Access to a regular bus service would have been particularly important for travelling safely in the evening.

Her work for the ELFS St. Leonard's Street Mother and Baby Clinic was probably the most conventional of her activities outside the home. But the ability to move freely in the streets without automatically attracting disapproval must have eased her on her way around East London in pursuit of the more revolutionary activities she undertook on behalf of the Federation, such as selling the **Woman's Dreadnought** and recruiting.

If she had any time for something more frivolous, the number 8 bus route from the garage, would have transported her "up West" to enjoy shopping in the department stores on Oxford Street, take tea with friends at the Lyon's Corner House at the Strand Palace Hotel or go to the theatre on Shaftesbury Avenue on a family outing.

Seeking refreshment and keeping company outside the home on Fairfield Road was still problematic for a woman. The road supported two pubs, the Bromley Arms and the Caledonian Arms, where Rosaline would not have been welcome on her own, or even in the company of other women, in the years running up to the First World War. Any woman entering a pub alone would immediately have been identified as a prostitute, drunkard or both. Some of these attitudes were beginning to change and some married women of the time could go for a drink on a Saturday night without risking social stigmatisation, provided they accompanied their husbands. However, the two pubs, both converted into flats now, must have brought a bit of life and colour to the street, if only for the men.

Although motor buses were commonplace, very few motor cars were in private ownership and suppliers of goods and services still relied on the horse and cart and bicycles to make deliveries. Women like Rosaline, who were in charge of a household, also made much more use of deliveries to the home to shop for groceries such as meat, and milk arrived in a horse-drawn "milk pram" laden with churns.

The horses, carts, and buses created a noisy, messy street scene which made Fairfield Road a more sociable environment, where women at home had plenty of opportunities during the day to chat with tradesmen and their neighbours on the front-door step.

However, Fairfield Road was also the location of significant monuments to East London's long history as an incubator of poverty, labour unrest and philanthropy, despite the predominantly lower-middle-class status of its residents in their flat-fronted terraces.

The Poplar Union at numbers 7–9 dispensed state aid, or "outdoor relief" to indigent members of the population according to the strictures of the Poor Law, a system established in 1601, now breaking at the seams, which would only disappear with the advent of the Welfare State in 1948.

In 1890 the Viscountess Clifden converted three terraced houses, numbers 75-79, into a hostel and restaurant for young women to give them something better than their employer provided during the working day at the Bryant and May match factory, in the hope that this improved environment would have an improving effect on their uncouth ways, as she perceived them.

Rosaline saw the Poplar Relief Station every day, a constant reminder of the social deprivation experienced by many other East Enders. The presence of the Clifden Institute and the Bryant and May Factory must have evoked memories of how seemingly powerless women, in possession of little formal education, could organise themselves and stand up against powerful industrialists to win better pay and conditions and become pioneers of the trade union movement. Their strike took place in 1888, as she attained her eighteenth year, and it surely left its mark on a woman who was to become an outstanding member of the East London Federation of Suffragettes.

SOURCES

Grace's Guide to British Industrial History: London General Omnibus Company
https://www.gracesguide.co.uk/London_General_Omnibus_Co

Gutzke, D. Gender, Class, and Public Drinking in Britain During the First World
https://hssh.journals.yorku.ca/index.php/hssh/article/viewFile/16578/15437

Kelly's Directory 1911

Koven, S. *The Heiress and the Matchgirl*. Princeton University Press 2015.

ARTICLE 4

Rosaline and Herbert

Rosaline married Herbert James McCheyne in 1896 when they were both 26 years old. By 1911 they had three children, Robert, 14, Georgina, two and Donald six months*.

Many women of the era married older men who could expect to exercise complete control over every aspect of family life. Rosaline's freedom to devote so much time to the East London Federation of Suffragettes in its earlier years suggests that Herbert did not actively oppose her life outside the domestic sphere.

The McCheynes also differed from many other East End Families in raising just three children, when huge families of seven to twelve or more were pretty much the norm. It is impossible to say why Rosaline and Herbert had such a small family but it's worth remembering that attitudes towards family planning were changing in the early twentieth century, while contraceptives** and educational material*** were becoming more freely available.

We might view sharing the terraced house in Fairfield Road (which still stands there today) with her husband, three children and another adult (possibly a lodger or relative) as a bit of a squeeze, but it would have made a striking contrast to the conditions endured by many other families in the area. It was not unusual to find a family of maybe thirteen packed into two rooms in a crowded tenement building, where all the residents shared one toilet, and one tap in the courtyard served all their household needs.

The McCheynes also enjoyed an unusual degree of financial security, when most families survived on the low wages paid to men in the docks and factories for dangerous, casual work. Herbert had a steady job as Woodwork Instructor with the Technical Educational Panel of the London County Council.

As an active member of the East London Suffragettes, Rosaline spent many hours engaged in activities outside the home. She worked at the St. Leonard's Street Baby Clinic and the Bromley ELFS office. She attended ELFS' meetings regularly and was the Joint Honorary Secretary of the Social Committee. She recruited new members and collected subscriptions. She sold the **Woman's Dreadnought** and bailed out her fellow suffragettes when they were arrested and held at Bow Police Station.

She must have been an admirable woman – industrious, generous and altruistic – but without detracting from these special qualities, she also had some advantages which distinguished her from many of her East End sisters.

She wasn't worn out by repeated childbirth and bringing up an enormous family with all the drudgery entailed, so she had energy to spare for ELFS.

Women of the labouring poor often had to work during their husbands' regular spells of unemployment and many went out charring in other women's homes. Thanks to Herbert's safe job and steady income, there was no need for Rosaline to take paid employment, so she had time to commit herself to the cause.

It would be gratifying to imagine that Rosaline also benefited from the approval of a supportive husband in her work for ELFS but, at this point, Herbert's life and disposition are almost entirely hidden from us.

SOURCES

* Census of 1911.

** Cook H. 2004. *The Long Sexual Revolution: English Women, Sex and Contraception 1800–1975*. Oxford University Press.

*** *Fruits of Philosophy* written by Charles Knowlton first published in England in 1877.

ARTICLE 5

On the Home Front with Rosaline

In 1913 as the mother of three children, landlady and mistress of a comparatively spacious early-Victorian house, no one would have expected Rosaline to do anything but absorb herself completely in the mountains of domestic labour that went with each of these roles:

Sweeping, dusting and polishing floors, furniture and ornaments; supplying the kitchen range and fires in the parlour, dining room and bedrooms with coal; blacking the range; washing indoor floors and whitening outdoor steps; washing and drying clothes, towels, tea cloths, table and bed linen; cleaning the bath, sinks, scullery and lavatory; shopping for food and household products; cleaning windows inside the house; cooking breakfast and dinner for six; making beds every day, stripping them and changing the linen fortnightly; ironing and starching clothes and linen; mending and darning clothes, table and bed linen; washing dishes, pots, pans, glasses and cutlery after every meal; managing the household budget; dealing with tradesmen and delivery boys.

The list is overwhelming and there are probably omissions. This herculean undertaking was achieved with a limited supply of hot water provided by the range and a never-ending fight against trails of coal-dust.

There were no detergents to help dissolve grime and grease before removing it from floors, surfaces and dishes. Floors and steps had to be washed on hands and knees using a scrubbing brush.

Washing clothes and linen was hard physical work, using water heated by a copper boiler in the scullery, soap, a washboard for scrubbing and a wringer or mangle for squeezing water from the washing before it could be hung out to dry in the garden or yard, if you were lucky enough to have one. Successful drying depended entirely on the vagaries of the London weather.

Rosaline was fortunate. She could probably have afforded soap, and coal to heat the water needed for housework. Her home was not overcrowded or insanitary because of inadequate plumbing. She was, therefore, less likely to have battles with bedbugs, unlike her neighbours housed in the mean terraces and squalid tenements of Bow. Many ordinary homes were being connected to mains gas in this era to fuel the new gas stoves which made cooking easier than on a temperamental, coal-fuelled range.

It's difficult to imagine how Rosaline combined the demands of managing a household with her life as an activist without some kind of help. Maybe her family went into the world a little less scrubbed and starched than their peers. Perhaps she employed one of the many married, working women of the East End who went out charring for women of every social class, including their own, to keep some money coming in during their husbands' periodic bouts of unemployment, when there was no work to be had in the factories and docks.

Rosaline had more than enough to fill her life at 55 Fairfield Road, but in 1913 she joined the East London Federation of Suffragettes and soon became indispensable to its cause. Her work as Joint Honorary Secretary for the Social Committee, volunteering at the Bromley Office and St. Leonard's Street Baby Clinic and campaigning on the streets of East London are a testimony to her diligence, determination and courage.

SOURCE

Victorian and Edwardian Services (Houses) 1850-1914. University of the West of England.

https://fet.uwe.ac.uk/conweb/house_ages/services/print.htm

ARTICLE 6

A Day in the Life of an Activist in 1914

We asked one of ELFS' first recruits, Mrs. Rosaline McCheyne, to tell us about a day in her life. Mrs. McCheyne is known by all as one of our hardest workers, so her report is of interest to all our members and busy women everywhere.

Here is her account in her own words:

I'm up with the lark every day, getting breakfast ready for the family, my husband Herbert, three children, Bob, Georgie and Don and my brother-in-law, George who's in lodgings with us. Before the war we'd have something like a nice kipper or sausages, but now it's just porridge. Still, it fills you up and there's less cooking and dishes to do. Don still likes his milk and biscuits. He's three and a half, so just a baby really. They're all off to work or school by half past eight and that leaves me and Don on our own at home.

On a Monday Mrs. Murphy from down the road arrives with her Jack, who's the same age as Don, to give me a hand with the washing. The bed linen is already soaking in the copper, and all the other clothes are piled up in the scullery waiting to be washed when she gets here. We spend the whole morning scrubbing, rinsing and wringing. Mrs. Murphy is a godsend. If she didn't come, I'd spend the whole day up to my elbows in soap and water. Little Don and Jack play together in the kitchen or, in good weather, out in the garden, where we can keep an eye on them both. On a good day, we have all the washing pegged out on the line by noon.

Bob and my little girl Georgie both come home for their dinner, and sometimes Herbert does too. I always ask Mrs. Murphy and Jack to stay and have a little bit with us too. I'm sure they don't eat enough, what with trying to manage on her man's army allowance. It's barely enough to keep body and soul together and that's when she gets it on time. This week we had a bit of a treat, some lovely, cold brisket left over from the Sunday roast, bubble and squeak and mustard pickle on the side, with jam roly poly and custard for afters.

If there's time after doing the dishes Mrs. Murphy and I have a quick natter over a cup of tea, then it's time to get my coat and hat on and off to the ELFS Bromley district office. First I take Don next door to stay with Mrs. Hutchings, who looks after him until his dad or brother, Bob, gets home in the evening. My Georgie goes to her house too after school and Mrs. Hutchings usually does their tea. She likes to have them by her as she has no children of her own.

It takes about ten minutes to walk to the office, but if it's too wet or very cold I take the motor bus. Mrs. Mantle and I have run the office for nearly two years and work very well together. There's quite a lot of post to sort out on Monday, so we divide it up between us and answer any letters. We then get on with our own special duties. I spend a lot of time dealing with the sale and distribution of our newspaper, the **Woman's Dreadnought**. This means making sure there are enough pitches where it can be sold and finding spots where no one will try to stop us. I also recruit the sellers and make sure they are all in the right place at the right time. This isn't as simple as it might sound.

I'm not one to blow my own trumpet but Bromley has a fine record, and sells more newspapers than any of the other districts. I try to take a pitch on Saturdays and aim to sell around twenty eight papers. I enjoy it, and passing the time of day with people as they stop by gives me a chance to get them to join ELFS. This is much harder since the war, as a lot of the women who'd like to join just cannot afford the subscription.

I see a lot of these women on the days I work at the Mother and Baby Clinic in St. Leonard's Street. They cannot even afford to feed their babies. They bring in these poor, grey little mites who look like skinned rabbits. Well, at least we are able to give them the free milk, and it warms my heart to see them fill out and turn pink as they ought to be, once they start getting proper regular feeds.

Anyway, not everyone is pleased to see us selling the newspaper or campaigning for votes for women on the street. Some of them think it's a scandal and they don't mind letting us know! A few of them can be quite rough but the local shopkeepers won't stand for anyone who threatens us. The others usually come round with a quiet word or a joke, even if they will never become supporters of our cause.

I also do the bookkeeping for the Bromley district and keep tabs on our bail fund. Our last May Day procession* taught me the importance of plenty of donations towards the kitty. So many members of Mrs. Pankhurst's bodyguard were arrested in Victoria Park when they tried to save her from being put back inside Holloway. I spent all that Sunday evening down at Bow Police Station bailing them out. Some went to prison gladly, but women with no one else to depend on at home had to be released for the sake of their children.

If there's a committee meeting in the evening, I go straight there after we've closed the office. I like to attend as often as I can, so that I can get all the news about what's happening at headquarters and in the other districts. Now that it gets dark so early at this time of year, I take the motor bus home from Old Ford Road to my house in Fairfield Road. Sometimes my eldest, Bob comes to meet me. I tell him not to, but he says he just wants to look after his dear old mum!

Well, as you can imagine, after a day like this, I'm done in. The first thing I do when I get in is to check that Georgie and Don have settled down for the night. Then Herbert and I sit in front of the fire and have a nice cup of cocoa before retiring to bed.

SOURCES

*'An Account of the Mayday Procession of 24th May', The *Woman's Dreadnought*, front page, 30th May, 1914

Committee Meeting Minutes of the East London Federation of Suffragettes, 28th February 1914–21st February 1916, transcribed by Rosemary Lucas for the Women's Hall Exhibition.

Housing and work pages on Pat Cryer's website: http://www.1900s.org.uk

Rosaline's words, as imagined by the author, were written in the way that someone of her era and education might have spoken, and her descendant was happy to see them appear in this form.

ARTICLE 7

Woman's May Day, 24th May, 1914

"Russian Methods in Victoria Park"

"I'll break your bloody arm and twist your bleeding neck"

This was the vile language used by one of His Majesty's Police Force against a woman fighting to protect Miss Sylvia Pankhurst as she was led away from Victoria Park to prison.

According to witnesses, once Miss Pankhurst was being driven away to Holloway in a taxi, the police lost control of themselves and resorted to acts of callous brutality against the women and men who had formed her bodyguard.

They pulled the women's hair, punched them in the face and twisted their arms. One police constable, K1129, stood out from the rest in his cruel treatment of one woman, whose thumb he bent back while twisting her arm behind her back. Aware of her helpless position, he taunted her with these words: "Kick me now, why don't you, kick me".

One officer, Inspector Beeton, showed some decency by urging his men to exercise restraint and offering to send for a doctor to tend to PC K1129's victim, a gesture which she declined with asperity.

Her defiance was typical of the spirit shown by the members of Miss Pankhurst's bodyguard before her arrest. Chained to her and each other, they stood fast as police smashed the chain which bound them to her with their truncheons.

The day had begun with high hopes for a splendid festival to be held in celebration of the women's suffrage movement.

Despite the rainy weather, Poplar and Canning Town raised a good muster which processed to 400 Old Ford Road, waving flags and bearing banners aloft, where they were joined by Miss Pankhurst, her bodyguard and the Bromley and Bow contingent.

As Miss Pankhurst and her bodyguard of twenty approached Victoria Park, events took a dramatic turn. They were confronted with mounted police who drove them into the boating enclosure and locked them in, whereupon fifty men of the police and CID set about them in a prelude to the ugly scenes described above.

Surely, such methods are more fitting to Cossacks attacking the Russian people, than the English police in dealing with their fellow citizens?

Some witnesses averred that the police had drafted in case-hardened officers from other districts, inclined to be less scrupulous in their treatment of people of the East End of London, while others claimed that police infiltrated the crowd with officers disguised as costermongers. East End women, they say, can smell a detective.

Meantime outside Victoria Park, police with batons drove back festival-goers as well as others who wished to visit the park, as they usually did on a Sunday. One such angry visitor instigated a fist fight which led to the opening of the park gates.

Despite Miss Pankhurst's arrest, the festival turned out to be a tremendous success. Nine platforms, decorated with flowers, hosted speakers from groups as diverse as The Actresses' Franchise League and The Forward Cymric Suffrage Union.

The Votes for Women speeches drew the greatest numbers and stirred the greatest general excitement. Converts were made to the cause, including a prize fighter who had come along to oppose it. The day ended in triumph, with a vote for a resolution demanding votes for women being carried unanimously by the crowd.

Adapted from the front page of the *Woman's Dreadnought*, 30th May, 1914

Afterword

"**A Day in the Life of an Activist**", Article 6, and the account of the May Day procession, Article 7, of 1914 highlight two very different approaches to activism.

There is Sylvia Pankhurst, surrounded by her bodyguard, eloquent and vociferous, always on the front line and in the headlines. A lifelong campaigner for social justice, she lives on in the records she made of her own words and the histories written by others.

Then, there is Rosaline McCheyne. Her participation in ELFS formed a brief period in her life and has almost been forgotten, but she is an exemplar of the quiet activist, the sort of woman who ends up as an "unsung heroine". Her dedication to ELFS' more mundane activities wove part of the mesh which held the organisation together from day to day, while others occupied the limelight.

I hope this collection will shine a little light on the contribution she made to improving women's lives at a turning point in the history of their struggle for equality.

Anne Padfield is rightly proud to count her among her ancestors.

Acknowledgements

My heartfelt thanks go to Andrew Hayler who supported me in every way as this work progressed.

I began the research for it as a volunteer for the **The Women's Hall Exhibition** staged at the Tower Hamlets Local History Library and Archive in 2018, and I would like to thank Lauren Sweeney, Volunteer Manager, for making the experience such a pleasure, as well as the library staff for their assistance and Tamsin Bookey, Heritage Manager, for suggesting writing up Anne's interview as a permanent record for the library.

Anne Padfield gave very generously of her time to tell the story of Rosaline and her family and answer all my questions in the months after our interview. She also provided the family photos which appear in the text. The knowledge she shared helped to confirm some of my assumptions about Rosaline and dispel others, when I was itching to know about her life after ELFS, and enlivened the story I wanted to tell.

Vera Brice used her years of experience and expertise in book design to produce the elegant publication you hold in your hand, without asking anything in return.

Caroline Hotblack's meticulous proofreading resulted in a vastly improved text and gave me a crash course in many fine points of grammar, punctuation and the use of English, which I was previously unaware of.

Caroline and Nicola Scott both lent a listening ear as the work progressed, and Nicola patiently heard out my first vague ideas about what to include in the text and how to present it. Rebecca Mulligan kindly undertook the final read through and provided invaluable feedback on the readability of the text.

The cover image of Rosaline and the mothers and babies standing together outside the clinic, which she ran at 53 St. Leonard's Street, is a photograph taken by Norah Smyth. Norah's pictures of ELFS in action between 1913–1916 are held in the collection of Estelle Sylvia Pankhurst's papers at the International Institute of Social History, Amsterdam. Tamsin Bookey provided a copy of the photo from the local history library's digital collection and it was reproduced with the kind permission of Paul Isolani Smyth, great nephew of Norah Smyth, pioneering woman photorapher, suffragette and philanthropist.

Lightning Source UK Ltd.
Milton Keynes UK
UKHW020727050123
414875UK00014B/744